ELOQUENCE

THE PRINCIPLES OF ELOQUENCE

Together with examples selected from the works of the most famous orators of ancient and modern times

BY

NIKOLAUS SCHLEINIGER, S.J.

Revised and enlarged by KARL RACKE, S.J.

Translated from the Sixth German Edition

BY

JOSEPH SKELLON

(FORMERLY MASTER AT BEAUMONT COLLEGE)

With Preface by F. KING, S.J.

KEGAN PAUL, TRENCH, TRÜBNER & CO
DRYDEN HOUSE
43 Gerrard Street, Soho, London, W
1909

Tot nos praeceptoribus, tot exemplis instruxit
antiquitas, ut possit videri nulla sorte nascendi
aetas felicior quam nostra, cui docendae priores
elaborarunt.

Quint. 12, 11, 22.

Imprimatur

Friburgi Brisgoviae, die 3 Ianuarii 1905.

✠ THOMAS, Archiepps.

Cum opus, cui titulus est: *Grundzüge der Beredsamkeit*, a Nicolao Schleiniger, sacerdote Societatis Iesu compositum et a Carolo Racke S.J. elabo-
ratum (editio VIa) aliqui eiusdem Societatis revisores, quibus id commissum
fuit, recognoverint et in lucem edi posse probaverint, facultatem concedimus,
ut typis mandetur, si ita iis, ad quos pertinet, videbitur.
In quorum fidem has litteras manu nostra subscriptas et sigillo muneris
nostri munitas dedimus.

Exaten, d. 4 Octobris 1904. (L. S.) P. C. SCHAEFFER,
Prov. Germ. Praepositus.

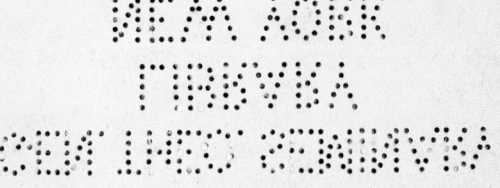

Letchworth : At the Arden Press

PREFACE TO THE FIRST EDITION

THE object of this work is to give a theoretical and practical exposition of the general rules of rhetoric, so that, first, they may be of service to all students; and, secondly, act as a foundation to such as intend to specialize in the art of oratory.

Our main endeavour has been to develop the true nature and essence of eloquence, as opposed to mere declamation, in short, yet comprehensive and well-defined outlines, illustrated by means of suitable and carefully chosen examples. In particular we have endeavoured to give prominence to the psychological value of eloquence: when this has once been grasped and then kept constantly in view, as the guiding star, not only will the theory be considerably simplified, but it will be denuded of a certain complexion of pedantry, of which it is not always innocent, and attain the perfection of an art. Thus it will be a most powerful factor in enabling the student to make a practical use of the natural talent latent in him. This will be developed from its roots, tended and trained until fruits are produced, which will endure long after all remembrance of the various processes has vanished.

Although it was our original intention to give only a synopsis of the main rules of eloquence, we have, on further consideration, thought it better to treat several of them at length: this applies especially to those sections dealing with *arrangement* and the *emotions;* for they are the very foundation of the art, and hence require careful study.

Unlike most authors, we think the *topics* worthy of much study and not as mere useless relics of antiquity; hence, we have discussed them at length and given many examples in illustration. Our reason for this will be stated in the proper place. We have also endeavoured to show the importance of a proper use of figurative language.

ELOQUENCE

Under the conviction that true eloquence can only flourish when it draws its nourishment from classical sources, and, that in this matter, as much depends on well-authenticated principles as on genuine examples, we have imitated the teaching of past ages of the learned, and based our theory on that as taught by Cicero and Quintilian; at the same time we have given full consideration to modern writers. Our illustrations are taken mainly from those two great orators, who, in the opinion of all generations, stand at the head of their art, namely, Demosthenes and Cicero; to these we have also added copious extracts from speeches of more recent date. Many writers have been in the habit of selecting their examples at random, without regard either to unity of purpose or suitability of style, culling now from letters, now from poetry or narrative. Such a proceeding is more likely to ruin the style of the student than to form it; it has helped, not a little, to obliterate the true idea of the nature, of the spirit and of the language of eloquence, and to debase it to the level of mere showy declamation. True, we occasionally find, in historical and poetical works, passages of an oratorical value, for there exists, of course, an epic and an historic eloquence; but the above remarks refer only to the choice of passages, quite outside the sphere of the poet or the prose writer.

We have not gone particularly into the theory of the various branches of eloquence, because (excepting always pulpit eloquence) we consider they are all guided by the same general rules; to the law-student a knowledge of the practise and procedure of the law-courts of his native country will give far more solid help than any mere theory gleaned from rhetorical works; and the same may be said in regard to the political speaker and an acquaintance with political circumstances. The most that theory can do for them is to point out the peculiar character of the different classes of oratory, and this we have endeavoured to do in the present work.

We trust that the object we have proposed to ourselves, namely, the exposition, in a clear and forcible manner of the true spirit of eloquence, for the benefit of students, may

PREFACE

be attained; and that these pages may put fresh vigour into the study of the rules of oratory, and render it easy, practical and crowned with success.

Nikolaus Schleiniger, S.J.

PREFACE TO THE SIXTH EDITION

I HAVE endeavoured to perfect the work according to the spirit of its author. In the main it is the same; whatever changes there are, either small or great, must justify themselves. The copious use made by the author, both in the theoretical and practical parts, of old classical literature, has been retained. Apart from the undeniable significance of the rhetoricians and orators drawn upon, the scheme of the book, out of regard for the wishes of readers and the particular desire of the author have influenced me in this matter.

The "selected passages" have been much increased. Examples from living orators, after long consideration, have not been included. It will be unnecessary to state that the author does not intend any slight by this decision.

KARL RACKE, S.J.

Exaten, Dutch Limburg,
  December 15, 1904.

PREFACE TO THE ENGLISH TRANSLATION

THE design of the present translation is to supply a want which so far has received but little attention in English-speaking countries. Many people here receive so much of a classical education as to be familiar with at least the names and some of the works of the Latin and Greek writers, but their training has just fallen short of that which would have given a human interest to the study.

The gift of speech is pre-eminently the prerogative of man, the clearest medium of communication between minds, the study of it the one pursuit which brings us into the closest contact with our fellow-men, for speak we must, unless we be hermits; and whether we address a crowded senate or utter a remark to a chance acquaintance, alike we are under the necessity of making our thought clear, removing prejudice or conciliating good will. Like all other gifts, it can be cultivated; and those have the best opportunities for perfecting themselves in this gift, or, at least, of acquiring an intelligent appreciation of it as exercised by others, who have had the advantage of being introduced to the works of those whose discourses have survived the test of time and changing fashion. During the years when the energies were absorbed in the mere mechanical task of acquiring the languages, there was little time or energy to investigate the principles which lie at the back of all good use of words; this book is intended to stimulate that interest, and to give the scientific ground on which a good literary judgement may be formed. To attain this result in the shortest and most efficacious manner, the principles are enunciated and illustrations given of them from the approved sources; and in order that the interest may not be confined to the writers of antiquity, examples are drawn also from comparatively modern authors. It is hoped in this way to minister to the wants of those who have felt that their education in the classics, as happens so often nowadays, was confined to the consideration of philological questions, with a consequent detraction from the far more interesting side of the literary quality of the authors they read.

F. KING, S.J.

Manresa House, Roehampton, S.W.

NOTE BY THE TRANSLATOR

IN the English version special prominence has been given to British and American requirements, and numerous extracts from the speeches of orators of both nations have been added. Many of the extracts from American speeches have, by the kind permission of the publishers, been gathered from *The World's Famous Orations*, published by Messrs Funk and Wagnall, of New York and London.

London, October, 1908.

CONTENTS

INTRODUCTION

PART I

xj

ELOQUENCE

CONTENTS

CONTENTS

ELOQUENCE

ELOQUENCE

INTRODUCTION

I. Eloquence: its Essence and Divisions

ELOQUENCE is a part of the wider subject of the art of speech, that is, the art of expressing, in appropriate language, the thoughts, feelings and wishes of the soul. Corresponding to the three functions of language, to instruct, to entertain or to convince, Eloquence, in its fullest sense, embraces every method of presenting thought in a way calculated to secure one or other of these objects (*didactic prose, poetry, eloquence*). It meets us under the most diverse forms, in the measured speech of the statesman, the minute exposition of the pleader, in the lightning dialectic of the controversialist, and the moving address of the missioner, in the lively narration of the story-teller and the compelling images of the poet. At one time it sways an audience in the vibrating tones of the speaker, at another it whispers to the reason in the silent influence of the written word.

Here we will confine ourselves to Eloquence in the strict sense of the term. This, if we consider the word in itself, is the power to persuade. To persuade is to convince by exhortation, or to touch by means of the living word; as a matter of fact, to move others to a decision, to guide their wishes and desires in a given direction is the object of the orator, and just so far as a speech succeeds in this is it a work of eloquence. According to its aim, therefore, we can define Eloquence as *the art of speaking in such a manner as to win over others to a particular point of view.** The speaker's instru-

*So also many explain Cicero's words, "Sit orator nobis is, *qui accommodate ad persuadendum* possit dicere" (De Orat. 1, 61, 260). No exact definition has been given by Cicero of this *persuadere*, and a close study of his rhetorical works gives one the idea that he himself had no clear notion of his art. Aristotle defines it as: ἔστω ἡ ῥητορικὴ δύναμις περὶ ἕκαστον τοῦ θεωρῆσαι τὸ

ment is *the living word*; (a speech such as Cicero's Second Philippic, which from the very beginning is only meant to be read, has no reality in it). How the "word" is to be handled, so that it may have the power to turn the opinions of others in the direction desired by the orator, will be examined later on.

Eloquence is, in the first place, a gift of nature. When a man is bent upon winning over others to his opinions for some special end, he calls forth the whole strength of his abilities and puts into his *words* all the light of his mind and the glow of his heart. Nature endows him with the gift of eloquence. But nature is developed by the use of fixed rules and so is brought to a higher perfection; hence Eloquence becomes an *art*, that is to say, an excellence resting upon well-known principles.

From this definition of the notion of eloquence it does not follow that every man who possesses the gift of merely graceful utterance has a claim to the art of eloquence. To the Greeks Eloquence was $\dot{\eta}$ δεινότης τοῦ λέγειν, originally something quite distinct from the art of elegant and chosen language, εὐστομία, εὐγλωττία, εὐέπεια (elegance of diction); it was among the later Rhetoricians, when all sorts of affectations and sophistics stunted the fair classic growth, and when ῥητορεύειν and σοφιστεύειν had become synonymous and degraded in meaning, that these expressions came into vogue to describe Eloquence.

Eloquence again is distinguished from poetry.*

The former has for its main object the True and the Good, the latter the Beautiful; the former appeals to the will,

ἐνδεχόμενον πιθανόν. In the accompanying explanation the περὶ ἕκαστον is emphasized as the characteristic feature. A more exact rendering of πείθειν (πιθανόν) is not given.

Cicero, and quite rightly, too, places the chief point of Eloquence in this *accommodate* dicere, and *not* in the result (*persuadere*), because a speech may be very eloquent and yet not bring about the desired effect. True eloquence merely requires that the speech should comply with all the conditions *requisite* for gaining the object in view.

* On this point, cf. Sulzer's Theorie der schönen Kunste und Wissenschaften: Grenzen der Beredsamkeit ; Schott, Die Theorie der Beredsamkeit mit besonderer Anwendung auf die geistliche Beredsamkeit, bd. I. kap. 4.

How, moreover, the three elements here mentioned, the rhetorical, the poetical and the philosophical, like neighbouring powers, not only frequently

the latter to the imagination and the feelings; the stirring up of the æsthetic sense—the *delectare*—is the poet's aim, while for the speaker it is only a means.

The speaker is also distinct from the philosopher. The latter's task is to search out and discover the truth, which, so far as he can impart it, he tries to convey to the understanding of his hearers. The speaker too aims at a knowledge of the truth, at the same time that he tries to force upon his hearers a practical adoption of it, and so, after appealing to the understanding, he proceeds at once to work upon the feelings and the will. The philosopher moreover considers the Good singly from the point of view of its objective reality, i.e., under the aspect of Truth, and thus even the practical or moral philosopher ever remains in the domain of speculation; the speaker, on the contrary, regards the Good in relation to an immediately practical object, in its application to life; for him the philosophic development is only a stage in his progress; his ultimate goal is some practical decision.

2. *Divisions of Eloquence.* The older rhetoricians with Aristotle * considered the audience under the aspect of judge or citizen, or merely as impartial onlooker—θεωρός; according to these three standpoints they made three divisions of eloquence, forensic, political, deliberative (genus deliberativum, judiciale, demonstrativum seu exornativum), this last including the panegyric and the invective. † At the present day the usual division is into profane (political, forensic, military, academic), and sacred or pulpit eloquence (homiletic).

invade each other's provinces, but strive to unite in the accomplished speaker, though in different proportions, may be seen in many of the most beautiful examples of oratorical talent. See, for example, on this point Frederick Schlegel: Gesch. d. alten u. neuen Literatur, 2 th. 13 vorles. in Bezug auf Bossuet.

* Ἀνάγκη δὲ τὸν ἀκροατὴν ἢ θεωρὸν εἶναι ἢ κριτήν· κριτὴν δὲ ἢ τῶν λεγενημένων ἢ τῶν μελλόντων. Ἔστι δ' ὁ μὲν περὶ τῶν μελλόντωτν κρίνων, οἷον ἐκκλησιαστής (citizens in the people's assembly)· ὁ δὲ ηερὶ τῶν γεγενημένων, οἷον ὁ δικαστής. ὁ δὲ τῆς δυνάμεως (intrinsic worth of the speech, talent of the orator) ὁ θεωρός. ὥστ' ἐξ ἀνάγχης ἂν εἴη τρια γένη τῶν λόγων τῶυ ῥητορικῶν, συμβουλευτικόν, δικανιόνκ δεικτικόν. (Arist. Rhet. 1, 3. Cf. Cic., Orat. partit. 3, 10).

† "Est igitur, ut dixi, unum genus, quo laus ac vituperatio continetur; sed est appellatum a parte meliore laudativum" (Quint., Inst. Orat. 3, 4, 12). To gain a true knowledge of the ideas the older rhetoricians had of Eloquence, especially of the πείθειν (πιθανῶς λέγειν), *persuadere*, the epideictic oration and their opinions upon it must be carefully considered.

In the region of profane eloquence, as a result of modern statecraft, the political speech (parliamentary and platform) occupies a very important position. Also the increased number of associations and debating clubs, with their various constitutions and objects, have caused a rich development in the deliberative and demonstrative styles.

In the law courts, it is true, eloquence no longer plays the important part it did in Athens and Rome, but it still understands how to make its influence felt there.

With regard to academic eloquence it must be observed that, as it does not aim at moving the feelings or the will, but rather at a tasteful presentment of some speculative object (an appeal, so to speak, to the cultivated intellect), it does not lie within the domain of Eloquence but rather in that of graceful diction. The external form, however perfected, changes nothing in essential character, whatever little influence may be exercised by the didactic or philosophic shape which the discourse may assume. Since the philosopher, the poet or the historian may be at one time or another a speaker, even the academic discourse may partake of some of the features of a speech. A sharp division of ideas is, nevertheless, very needful; it is incredible how greatly eloquence suffers through misapprehension of its fundamental character.

II—*Rhetoric: its Scope and Nature*

3. Although, in the main, Rhetoric depends upon natural ability and a true inborn talent for it, still a proper use of its precepts and expedients, such as may be learnt from careful study of the art, is of great help, and, indeed, indispensable, if mistakes are to be avoided and perfection acquired. Horace's remarks on the creations of the poetic art are very much to our purpose.

> Natura fieret laudabile carmen an arte,
> Quæsitum est: Ego nec studium sine divite vena,
> Nec rude quid possit video ingenium: alterius sic
> Altera poscit opem res, et conjurat amice.*

The same may be said of Eloquence.†

* Ars Poet. 408-411.

† Nay, Hugh Blair goes so far as to say, "It is certain that study and

INTRODUCTION

By training, however, it can, as we have mentioned above, become perfect craftsmanship.

The scientific training in the art of Eloquence is called *Rhetoric*. Its object is to develop and form the latent oratorical talent. The means to attain this result are (1) acquaintance with the theory of Eloquence; (2) study of the most eminent orators; (3) unremitting practice. Yet rhetoric will not make a great orator, if the candidate is wanting in natural gifts. These gifts, so far, at least, as perfection is concerned, must comprise sound judgment, a keen intellect, deep feeling, a vivid imagination, a good memory, but above all a great and noble soul: ἔχειν δεῖ τὸν ἀληθῆ ῥήτορα μὴ ταπεινὸν φρόνημα καὶ ἀγεννές;* and as regards the body, a pleasing and attractive exterior, powerful lungs, distinct articulation and a good voice.

The speaker, also, especially at the present day, over and above his natural gifts and rhetorical training, needs a secure groundwork of religious knowledge and fixed principles, as well as a familiarity with the laws of thought, an intimate knowledge of mankind,† and finally experience of those springs of the will which are most sensitive to the particular style of his eloquence.‡

Divisions of Rhetoric

4. According to Cicero three points are to be kept ever before the eyes of the orator, *what* he says, *when*, or on *what* occasion and *how* he says it "quid dicat, et quo quidque loco, et quomodo." §

Thus: rhetoric falls naturally into three divisions:

(1) The choice of the subject of the discourse;

(2) The arrangement of the discourse;

(3) The form of the discourse; and, since the composition is judged by the delivery, we may add

(4) The memorizing and delivery of the discourse.

discipline are more necessary for the improvement of natural genius in oratory than they are in poetry. Homer formed himself; Demosthenes and Cicero were formed by the help of much labour, and of many assistances derived from the labour of others" (Lectures on Rhetoric, Lect. xxxiv).

* Περὶ ὕψους, 9, 3. † Orat. 14, 13. ‡ Inst. 1, 2, cxv., n. 38.

§ Cf. d'Agueseau, Rede über die Menschenkenntnis beim Gerichtsredner. See Conclusion I.

ELOQUENCE

Before we begin to enlarge upon these points, let us give a short résumé of the history of Eloquence and Rhetoric.

III—*A Brief Review of the History of Eloquence and of Rhetoric*

A. Eloquence

5. In its first and simplest meaning, or considered as a gift, Eloquence is as old as human society. Historically its origin can be traced back only as far as it became in more or less degree a matter of art or training. We encounter it in all its glory among two ancient peoples—the Greeks and Romans. As a rule it precedes poetry and paves the way for a higher development of the latter, just as ordinarily the various kinds of prose grew out of the language of poetry, first historic prose, then that of the tribune. Among the Greek States Athens was especially famous for her eloquence. The democratic nature of her republican constitution and the freedom of debate allowed on all matters of public interest made the gift of words a mighty weapon in the hands of the demagogue. The importance of the subjects in debate, involving as they did the power and influence of Athens, stimulated great thoughts and large views. The very conflict of eminent speakers always tended to raise the art to higher perfection, and there was no great statesman but sought to win his laurels in this field: for instance, Solon, Pisistratus, Themistocles, Pericles, Alcibiades. The Alexandrian Canon of Callimachus presents us with the following ten orators: (*) Antiphon of Rhamnus at Attica (5th c. B.C.); Andocides, his contemporary; Lysias of Athens (444-379 B.C.) a son of the orator Cephalus of Syracuse; Isocrates (436-338), an Athenian and pupil of the rhetorician Gorgias; Isaeus (about 400 B.C.) of Chalcis; **Demosthenes** (about 385-322) of Pæanium in Attica, probably a pupil of Isaeus, the King of Greek eloquence; Æschines (390-314) of Athens, the famous rival of Demosthenes, according to Quintilian's opinion the first

---

* For a critical appreciation of this orator see Quintilian, 1, 12, and in Dionysius of Halicarnassus, περὶ τῶν ἀρχαίων ῥητόρων ὑπομνηματισμοί and Τῶν ἀρχαίων κρίσις, etc.; see also in the present work the Conclusion, especially the parallel drawn between Demosthenes and Cicero.

INTRODUCTION

Greek orator after Demosthenes; Lycurgus (about 396-328) of Athens, and friend of Demosthenes; also Hyperides (d. 322), contemporary of Lycurgus, said to be a pupil of Isocrates and Plato, whom Longinus in his *Treatise on the Sublime* considers, in some respects, Demosthenes's superior, especially in delicacy and irony; Dinarchus of Corinth (born 361), imitator of Demosthenes ($\Delta\eta\mu\sigma\sigma\theta\acute{\epsilon}\nu\eta\varsigma\ \acute{o}\ \kappa\rho\acute{\iota}\theta\iota\nu\sigma\varsigma$), who after the death of Demosthenes and Hyperides exercised considerable influence in Athens.

The artificial development of Attic eloquence had begun with Gorgias of Leontium in Sicily, who (427) opened the first school of rhetoric in Athens, and in his own time reaped fame by his florid extempore speeches, though at a later date he was looked upon as a mere declaimer. Lysias introduced a higher finish in the concise structure of the discourse and in loftiness and purity of diction, though he lacked the harmony of the period which Isocrates developed. Finally, Demosthenes united, with tempered proportion, boldness of thought to strength and harmony of language. After his death and the loss of her freedom Attic eloquence declined. Its noble and virile character sank into the mannerisms of Demetrius Phalereus (300) and the declamation of the Sophists, the verbose and weakly Asiatic style, and the allied, if less sensuous, Rhodian mannerism.*

Among later orators, the following have some reputation: John Chrysostom (Golden-mouthed) of Prusa in Bithynia (in the first and at the beginning of the second century A.D.); Tiberius Claudius Herodes Atticus of Attica, Consul at Rome (about 143 A.D.), an adept in improvisation; Aelius Aristides of Adrianople in Bithynia (also in the second century, A.D.); Themistius Euphrades (the Deliberator) of Paphlagonia (in fourth century at Constantinople); Libanius of Antioch (314-395) orator and rhetorician.

At Rome oratory had great obstacles to overcome. Not only could it gain but a partial hearing amid the clash of arms, but the stern sense of the Romans thought it neces-

---

* On the Attic, Asiatic and Rhodian styles and their champions see Quintilian, Inst. 12, 10. For further information on these styles and on the subject of Rhetoric from the time of Alexander down to Augustus cf. Father Blass, Die griechische Beredsamkeit u.s.w., Berlin, 1865.

sary to issue edicts against the opening of schools of Rhetoric, an action which could plead justification on account
of the methods of the Greek sophists who were the first
teachers at Rome. Hence, the most influential orators of the
first centuries owed their eminence more to the gifts of nature than to any training;* thus C. Cornelius Cethegus, Caius
Lælius, Corn. Scipio Africanus, Cato Major, Sempronius and
Caius Gracchus, C. Aurel. Cotta and especially L. Licinius
Crassus and M. Antonius (grandfather of the triumvir bearing the same name, the former distinguished by his gift of
exposition, the latter by the skilful disposition of his argument and the intensity of his emotion).† But when the Romans became better acquainted with the dialectic nimbleness
of the Greeks and the power conferred by a study of Rhetoric,
the passion for training flamed up all round, and it had its
complete justification in Cicero (106-43 B.C.), the worthy rival
of the greatest of the Greek orators. After Cicero there came,
though at a considerable distance, Hortensius, Cæsar and
Brutus, followed later by M. Val. Corvinus Messala (d. 9.
A.D.) Under the Cæsars, as with the Greeks in their deca-
dence, eloquence lost its essential moral characteristics, and
with them its loftiness, its warmth, its naturalness. A certain excess of poetical expressions, a delusive brilliance in
thoughts and words, a pointing of epigram, alliteration and
antithesis, above all affectation and striving after effect—
these are the features that marked the decline of the once
mighty eloquence of Rome. Since forensic eloquence became
henceforward the goal of the Rhetoricians, it may be fairly
concluded that the sphere of politics no longer enjoyed the
privilege of free speech; hence the whole of rhetorical training narrowed down to the groove of the demands of the law
courts—and being confined to school exercises on all sorts
of imaginary and involved cases (*Declamationes, controversiæ*)
became in time a sort of pedantic and sophistic trickery. As
a pleader and the panegyrist of Trajan, Pliny the Younger

* On this matter *Quintilian* says: Fuere quaedam genera dicendi conditione
temporum horridiora, alioqui magnam jam ingenii vim prae se ferentia.
(12, 10, 10.)

†See: Cic., Brutus s. de clar. orat. 37, Quint. 12, 10, 10.

INTRODUCTION

(62-114 A.D.) gained a not unmerited reputation; Quintilian, too, and Tacitus may here also receive honourable mention.*

Among nations of more modern times eloquence could only develop naturally where, after the formation of a cultured language, the state policy was favourable and sanctioned some degree of free speech. Such was the case in England, France, America and much later in Germany and in other nations, where trials were held in public, and the parliamentary system became part of the constitution. William Pitt, the elder, Earl of Chatham (1708-1778), Edmund Burke (1730-1797), Grattan (Irishman, 1746-1820), Fox (1749-1806), Sheridan (1751-1816), Canning (1770-1827), O'Connell (1775-1847) one of the greatest public speakers of all times, Brougham (1778-1859), Peel (1788-1850), Macaulay (1800-1859), Beaconsfield (1804-1881), Gladstone (1809-1898), Bright (1811-1889). Among American orators we have Patrick Henry (1736-1799), S. Adams (1722-1774), Washington (1782-1796), Jefferson (1743-1826), Nott (1773-1866), Prentiss (1808-1850), Webster (1782-1852), Clay (1777-1852), Baker (1811-1861), Beecher (1813-1887), Ingersoll (1833-1899), Garfield (1831-1888), Conkling (1829-1888), Grady (1851-1889). Among the most celebrated French speakers we have Mirabeau (1715-1789), Barnave (1761-1792), Maury (1746-1817), Lally-Tollendal (1750-1830), Cazalès (1752-1805), Vergniaud (1753-1793), Guizot (1787-1874), Berryer (1790-1868), Thiers (1797-1877), Montalembert (1810-1870). In modern times Spain has one famous name, Donoso Cortes (1809-1853). Since the commencement of the Parliamentary system in Germany we have Gerlach (1795-1877), Waldeck (1802-1892), Windthorst (1812-1891), Mallinckrodt (1821-1874). The four last named at the time of the "Kulturkampf" displayed in their character as defenders of the rights of the Catholic Church great oratorical talent. Their most celebrated opponents were Bismarck (1815-1868), Bennigsen (1824-1902), Lasker (1829-1884). Mention must also be made of the Austrians Leo Graf von Thun (1811-1888), Haynald

---

*See: Perrot, "L'éloquence politique et judiciare à Athènes." Jebb, The Attic orators from Antiphon to Isaeos (1876).

(1816-1891), Greuter (1817-1888), and the Swiss G. J. Baumgartner (1797-1869).

While Greek and Roman eloquence was dragging out the last remains of a miserable existence, there sprang up a new eloquence on a far higher plane, Christian or sacred eloquence, full of irresistible strength and fire. Though in most centuries this type displayed none of the external splendour of the old classic eloquence, and indeed at certain periods was entirely detached from it, still among the Apostles of all ages it developed, eclipsing all the triumphs of secular oratory by the marvellous spread of the faith, the awakening and strengthening of Christian life, the welding of whole nations into one people, proving the might of its divine origin.

The most famous preachers of past ages were; in the West: Ambrose (340-397), Leo the Great (d. 461), Augustine (354-430), Peter Chrysologus (fifth century), Gregory the Great (540-604), and if we include the soul of eloquence vibrating in the written word, Tertullian (b. about 160), Cyprian (about 200-258), Jerome (340-420), Salvian (fifth century); in the East: Origen (185-254), Gregory of Nazianzum, brother of Basil Macarius, the Egyptian (300-391), Cyril of Jerusalem (315-386), Cyril of Alexandria (d. 444), **Chrysostom** (347-407), Ephraem (d. 373); in the Middle Ages: Bernard (1091-1153), Bernardinus (1380-1444), Vincent Ferrer (1350-1419); among the Germans: Berthold of Regensberg (d. 1272) and Tauler (1290-1361), later Geiler of Kaysersberg (1445-1510).

In later times pulpit eloquence entered on a brilliant career in France when Bossuet (1627-1704), Fénelon (1651-1715), Massillon (1663-1742), etc., offered a lofty spiritual earnestness, a comprehensive unity of subject and a nobly-inspired language worthy of the greatest orators of former times. In Italy there appeared Segneri (1624-1694), Tornielli (1693-1752), Benini (1711-1778); in Spain: John of Avila (d. 1569), Louis of Granada (1504-1588), Francis Borgia (1510-1572), Estrada (1518-1584); in Portugal: Vieira (1608-1697); in Poland: Scarga (1536-1612). In Germany the following have a reputation: Hunolt (1691-1746), later Moser (1751-1780),

INTRODUCTION

Jeanjean (1727-1790), Al. Schneider (1752-1818), Gretsch (1753-1826), Colmar (1760-1818); in later times: Beith (1788-1876), Diepenbrock (1798-1853), Förster (1800-1821), Ketteler (1811-1877); M. Eberhard (1815-1876), Ehrler (b. 1833), Roh (1811-1872), Roder (1812-1887), Zobel (1815-1893), Rive (1824-1884), Löffler (1834-1902); in England: Cardinal Wiseman (1802-1865), Thomas Burke (1830-1883), Newman (1801-1890); among Protestant preachers: Jeremy Taylor (1613-1667), Blair (1718-1800), Sterne (1713-1768), Whately (1787-1863), Dr Chalmers (1780-1847), Spurgeon (1834-1892).

(B) *Rhetoric*

6. Quintilian has a wise observation: "Initium dicendi dedit natura, initium artis observatio" (3, 2); "Art has its root in nature, theory in experience.* Empedocles of Agrigentum (about 400-430 B.C.) and his pupil Korax are mentioned as the first who dictated rules for eloquence. Tisias, pupil of Korax, and Gorgias, pupil of Tisias, removed the school of rhetoric from Sicily to Athens, where others were also founded and an impetus given to their erection elsewhere. A very famous teacher of rhetoric was their pupil Isocrates (436-338 B.C.) The greatest Greek work on the theory of Rhetoric is Aristotle's (384-322 B.C.) *Treatise* Τέχνη ῥητορική † This is divided into three parts or books: the first of rhetorical arguments and their relation to the three kinds of eloquence; the second of the passions and habits as they affect the speaker and his audience, and the common places; the third of rhetorical exposition and action; finally, of the constituent parts of a speech. The work contains many practical hints drawn from experience, and displays a great knowledge of the human mind. By founding the art on reason and first principles, it has been the guide for all succeeding centuries in this subject, as has been the Poetics of Aristotle in the domain of poetry.‡ Other Rhetoricians of

---

* On the gradual growth of the theory of Rhetoric, cf. Quint., Inst. Orat. 31, and L. Spengel, Συναγωγὴ τεχνῶν s. artium scriptores.

† This is the work always referred to when Aristotle is quoted.

‡ Other rhetorical works of Aristotle mentioned by Diogenes Laertius (cf. also Cic., De Orat. 2, 38, and De in Rhet. 2, 2, 6) as also his Τεχνῶν συναγωγή

eminence are Antiphon (fifth century B.C.), Lysias, Theophrast (pupil and successor of Aristotle), Demetrius Phalereus (fourth century). The work ascribed to him under the title *On Expression*—Περὶ ἑρμηνείας—is really that of Demetrius of Alexandria; later Apollonius (Molon), who taught first at Rhodes, where flourished the so-called Rhodian school, which is falsely ascribed to Æschines; afterwards at Rome 81 B.C., where he was teacher to Cicero and Julius Cæsar. Dionysius of Halicarnassus, contemporary of Cæsar and Pompey, well known as a writer of history, flourished also as a rhetorician, though his treatise addressed to Echekrates has reached us only in an imperfect form—on the other hand we possess very many of his writings; Hermagoras (first century B.C.); Apollodorus; Theodorus (teacher of Tiberius); Hermogenes (under Marcus Aurelius); Longinus (213-273 A.D.), famous for the treatise attributed to him, *On the Sublime*, Περὶ ὕψους—one of the most eminent works on Rhetoric of the olden time; Libanius of Antioch, the teacher of St John Chrysostom, a brilliant professor at Constantinople —of his works we have a rhetorical course of speeches and declamations, as also the Analyses of the speeches of Demosthenes.

The first Latin school of Rhetoric in Rome (as we have observed already, the instruction in Greek Eloquence began much earlier) was opened by L. Gallus Plotius (88 B.C.) of Lyons, who counted Cicero among his hearers. The great Roman pleader has, however, left to us the most precious instructions on his art, cast generally in the form of dialogues. The most important of these are:

(1) *De Oratore ad Quintum fratrem.* The first book treats of the formation of the speaker, the second of the search for

---

are unhappily lost. The work known by the name of Rhetorica ad Alexandrum has been triumphantly vindicated for Anaximenes by Spengel (see his commentary). This Τέχνη (contrasted with the more philosophical work of Aristotle) gives us the best treatise on the Praxis (Methods) of the older orators, and in this respect is of great value to gain a knowledge of them; it is only to be regretted that these teachers of the theory as well as the practice of oratory, adopted whole-heartedly the principle that the (rhetorical) end justifies the (rhetorical) means to such an extent that their regard for truth and justice appears in a more than doubtful light.

and disposition of the matter, the third of oratorical expression and delivery. The whole work has a singular distinction of brilliancy and charm in its composition.

(2) *Orator seu de optimo genere dicendi* (ad Brutum); on the ideally perfect orator.

(3) *Brutus, seu de claris oratoribus;* a history of Roman eloquence. What the Rhetoric of Anaximenes was among the Greeks, that, among the Latins, is the work *Rhetorica ad Herennium*, at the time ascribed to Cicero, now with greater probability assigned to Cornificius. The most perfect and all-embracing theory in our opinion is that of Quintilian (born about 35 A.D.) who, in his work *Institutionis Oratoricæ libri duodecim,** with all his fund of experience and cultivated taste, follows the progress of the speaker from his first crude attempts to the very pinnacle of his art. On the other hand, the Declarations ascribed to him are not genuine. Finally, we must mention the dialogue rightly attributed to Tacitus† *De causis corruptæ eloquentiæ‡*. In later times we may make mention of Fénelon's three *Dialogues on Eloquence;* d'Aguesseau's *Discourse on the Decline of Forensic Eloquence;* Hugh Blair's *Lectures on Rhetoric;* Whateley's *Rhetoric;* A. Müller's *Twelve Lectures on Eloquence and its Decline in Germany;* Kleutgen's *Ars Dicendi*, and Philippis' *The Art of Oratory.*

The abundant literature on ecclesiastical rhetoric as also the particular history of sacred eloquence is fully treated of in a special work.

* This is the work alluded to always when Quintilian is quoted.

† Assigned by some to Quintilian, by others to the younger Pliny, and by others again to Suetonius.

‡ The Greek Rhetoricians were first edited by Walz, and lastly by Spengel, and the Latin Rhetoricians by Halm. Ioh. Ch. G. Ernesti, Gr. Technol. rhet., 1875, gives a good explanation of the technology of the older rhetoric. Volkmann's Rhetoric of the Greeks and Romans (1885) and Chaignet's La Rhétorique et son Histoire (1888) are deserving of special mention.

ELOQUENCE

PART THE FIRST

Discovery of the Matter (Inventio) *

7. The subject matter of this part naturally embraces the methods by which the arguments and motives (πίστεις, πιθανά; *argumenta persuasibilia*) may be found to win over the audience to the opinion of the orator. But first something must be said as to the *determination* of *the subject, the aim* and the *leading theme* of the discourse, for unless these points are settled, an effective employment of material is not possible.

SECTION I—*The Theme, Aim, Proposition*

8. *Theme.*—By Theme is understood the subject with which the speech deals.

In the first place a distinction must be made between the theme in its *wider*, and the theme in its *narrower* sense.

The former describes the subject in its *fullest* signification, and, by many it is simply named "Subject" (*materia*); the latter describes the subject according to the particular point of view of the orator; it is that portion of it of which he treats *quæstio*, ζήτημα (that which is sought).†

"Eloquence" is a theme in the wider sense of the word; "The great importance of Eloquence" a theme in the narrower sense. The standpoint from which the theme in the narrower meaning is viewed will determine the Manner of division. It is either *abstract* (*quæstio infinita*, Θέσις) or *concrete*, (*quæstio finita*, ὑπόθεσις). In the first case the subject is the *notion* of a species or kind, in the second of a particular individual or thing. A distinction must also be made between *theoretical*

---

*Εὕρεσις, παρασκευή. It is to be noted, once for all, that the old Rhetoricians employed different terms for the same object, while, on the other hand the same expressions did not always indicate the same thing.

†cf. Meunier, The Doctrine of the Matter of the Sermon; Kleutgen, Ars Dicendi, iv, 1, 1.

and *practical* (*quæstiones cognitionis* and *actionis*) simple and compound themes (*simplices, compositæ*). But of this later.

Very often the theme is offered by circumstances and determined beforehand.

If, however, it is left to the free choice of the orator, he must give careful attention to certain qualities necessary for a good theme. It must be: (1) *Suitable*, (2) *Uniform*, (3) *Limited*, (4) *Significant*.

(1) *Suitable*—first of all for the *purpose* the orator has in view; secondly, to the *person* of the orator, his age, his position, his abilities; thirdly, to his *audience* and their circumstances, needs, expectations, and in harmony with the exigencies of time and place.

> Sumite materiam vestris, qui scribitis, æquam
> Viribus, et versate diu, quid ferre recusent,
> Quid valeant humeri.*

The same advice which the poet here gives to the poet is also applicable to the orator; and, similarly, what Cicero says as to the tone of the speech applies also to the subject; "Nam nec semper, nec apud omnes, nec contra omnes, nec pro omnibus, nec omnibus eodem dicendum arbitror."†

(2) *Uniform*—The theme must have the quality of *Unity*,‡ that is, it must have no divisions, or, if there are any, they must be very intimately united; in other words, it must be either *simple*, or the association of ideas must be so close that the component parts form a unity. "Crime is the greatest of evils," "In thy breast are the stars of thy destiny," are simple themes, because they contain one simple undivided thought. "The duty and blessing of the observance of the Sunday" is a compound but still a united theme. It contains certainly two different thoughts which can be expanded into two sentences: The observance of Sunday a duty; the observance of Sunday a source of blessing. But these two truths are closely united

---

* Hor., Ars poet. 38.   † Cic., Orat. 35, 123.

‡ The reason why Rhetoricians insist on unity in the theme is *not*, as it would seem at first sight, on *æsthetic* grounds but for *practical* reasons. Indeed, a speech which lacks unity must lose in strength and effectiveness in proportion as the subjects increase. Unity of discourse is not possible without unity of theme, for the theme is the foundation of the speech. It cannot be denied that unity helps to impress upon the fabric of eloquence the stamp of beauty. St Augustine says (Ep. 18), "Omnis pulchritudinis forma, unitas est."

both by the unity of the subject (observance of the Sunday) and the unity of the object in view (exhortation to keep the Sunday holy).*

(3) *Limited*—The theme must also be *kept within the limits of the object in view*. It must neither be too overflowing with meaning, containing too many truths, nor must it be meagre or watery. If the subject chosen is too fertile, it cannot be properly worked out. The orator finds himself obliged rather to *point out* than to *unfold* his thoughts, consequently his speech will make little impression. He must, therefore, consider carefully which view of his subject he will treat of. In any case, within the narrow bounds of a speech, things can seldom be presented in their entirety; and if they could, it would not always be advisable, because this would not help the speaker to attain the end in view. Hence the demand for a judicious limitation. On the other hand, the subject must not be too narrow, or there will be a want of sufficient material, and the orator will be tempted during its development to overstep the mark; that is, he will seek refuge in meaningless phrases, academic dissertations, or wearying repetitions. It is true that by these means a patchwork of veneer may hide this poverty of mind and theme, but it will never remove the traces of inner worthlessness.

(4) *Significant*—Finally, the subject must be *pregnant with meaning and worthy of the consideration of the audience*. This follows from the nature and object of eloquence. Purely theoretical propositions, which bear neither directly nor indirectly upon the desires and actions of mankind, should not form the foundation of the speech. Neither are all matters of a practical nature appropriate for a theme. Trivial and unimportant matters are scarcely deserving of being treated in detailed speech.†

---

*In the language of Scholastic Philosophy this might be expressed as: The theme for one purpose treats of two formal objects by means of one material object.

† It is of importance for the young speaker to choose for his exercise only matters adapted for oratory. Thus the practice is not to be approved of, of giving, for exercises in the art of composing a speech, as too often happens, either wholly sentimental and idyllic subjects, which lend themselves but too easily to insipid sentimentality and nervous speech, or empty and meaningless themes, or any subjects which by their nature, or in their setting, are abstract

9. *Aim of the Speaker.* The development of the discourse is determined by the aim of the speaker, just as the architect settles his plan of erecting a building by the particular object to which the building is to be devoted; and as the musician in composing takes his keynote from the spirit which is to pervade his piece from the plot of the libretto, and from the effect to be produced by his music.*

Above all things the speaker must have his objective clearly before him. *This is of the highest importance,* since upon it turns the whole of the practical direction of the speech, and without this practical, clearly defined, and all-compelling directness, the discourse becomes merely a literary or philosophical essay. At times one single aim may be the goal of a series of speeches leading up to it, as we see in Demosthenes and Cicero: indeed, Demosthenes devoted his whole life to the great end of the independence of Greece, as O'Connell gave his for the freedom of Ireland. *It is the inspired grasp of the object which gives all the power to eloquence.*

"Pectus est quod disertos facit."

10. *The Proposition.* The immediate practical result of the consideration which the orator has given to the purposeful and afford no freedom of movement to the young mind. Among the last we may reckon the following : "What are the points of agreement and difference between morality and legislation?" "What is the peculiar value of the History of Philosophy?" "How is it that reference to God gives the highest moral value to our actions?" "Why is it appropriate that experimental psychology should be taught" in the top classes of our public schools? " Our attitude towards time," " Our cosmopolitan attitude," "The Ideal," " Probability," "Of arousing and encouraging a real interest for truth," etc. Such themes can, of course, exercise the thinking faculty of the young and afford matter for learned dissertations, but are quite unsuited for exercise in oratory. They stimulate an idea or feeling of eloquence, from the speculative not the practical side, and force the student, instead of addressing the minds and hearts of a living audience, either to drift into abstract philosophy, or, where there is want of thinking power, to expend himself in meaningless fine phrases. The worst of it is that he comes to regard such productions as eloquence, just because discourses more or less rhetorical in form are presented to him in collections of examples as products of eloquence.

* Sulzer well remarks—to introduce a third analogy—that, as the painter must not only represent his subject true to nature, but also in accordance with his special end in view; so the speaker should develop his subject in such a way as to produce the most powerful effect in teaching, in persuading or warning his audience; in other words *the best effect* in the *design* of his speech. (Theorie der Künste and Wissensch; Eigensch. des Redners).

comprehension of his subject finds expression in what Rhetoric terms *propositio*. In other words, the proposition is neither more nor less than the *expression* of the leading theme of the discourse *in one single sentence;* or, as Fénelon says, "The Speech in Brief." The discourse grows out of it as the flower from the bud, and the tree from the seed. If the proposition does not itself *clearly* express the object of the speech, still the outline or sketch of the object in view is usually contained in it: at times prudence may suppress both one and the other of these features, but in any case, the *speaker* must know quite clearly what his *aim and proposition is;* this must always be before his eyes, and this it is which determines the limits of the discourse, and endows it with the attribute of unity. Since then, the proposition is but the leading theme condensed into one single sentence, it follows that it must possess the selfsame qualities.

SECTION II. *Of the Means for the Practical Development of the Statement of the Subject of Discourse (Proposition)*

11. When a statement of theme appropriate to the object in view has been chosen, it must always be kept in mind in the process of development, for only in such case will there be reasonable grounds for hoping that the resulting discourse will make the desired impression upon the hearer. Hence, a thorough knowledge must be gained of the *oratorical aids;* that is of the *qualities* a speech must possess, if it is to have the effect of influencing the minds of an audience. According to Aristotle, these may be reduced to three heads: The first concerns the *personal character* of the orator (ἐν τῷ ἤθει τοῦ λέγοντος); the second, the *inducing of a certain disposition in the hearer*, (ἐν τῷ τὸν ἀκροατὴν διαθεῖναί πὼς); and the third, the *speech itself in so far as it demonstrates* or makes the *impression* of demonstrating (ἐν αὐτῷ τῷ λόγῳ, διὰ τοῦ δεικνύναι ἢ φαίνεσθαι δεικνύναι.* We encounter the same three divisions in Cicero, together with a rather valuable rearrangement, which we adapt to our needs. "Tribus rebus," says the Roman orator, "homines ad nostram sententiam

* Rhet. 1, 2, 3.

perducimus, aut docendo aut conciliando aut permovendo." *

But the three means are not to be employed quite in the same way. "Una ex tribus his rebus res præ nobis est ferenda," Cicero continues, "ut nihil aliud nisi docere velle videamur: reliquæ duæ sicuti sanguis in corporibus, sic illæ in perpetuis orationibus fusæ esse debebunt."

Our intention is to treat of the most important points of this threefold proposition, which the orator must always keep before his eyes, in the development of the matter of his speech, so we must consider:

(1) The means, by which the orator *instructs*.

(2) The oratorical devices and considerations by means of which he *prevails* and *captivates*.

(3) The emotions, which enable him to influence the *mind* and *heart*.

Such are the three steps which must be climbed if we desire to arrive at our goal.†

* Cic., De Orat. 2, 77, 310.
† Hence in other places " delectare" (Or. 21, 69 ; Br. 49, 185).

CHAPTER I

Rhetorical Aids by means of which the Speaker teaches

12. The essentials of teaching, i.e., of *such an exposition of the nature and meaning of a subject that the hearer is not only provided with a clear and accurate presentment of it, but also with an intimate conviction of its truth* are: the *explanation* of the subject and the *establishment* thereof on solid foundations.

The *explanation* is the gradual development of the truth, at least of the leading ideas or circumstances which bear in a special manner on the discourse, and would be obscure to the audience unless discussed. It is always, according to circumstances, an explanation of words or things. In historical subjects it is the facts of the case, a *verbal account* or *document*, or in cases where this rises to pictorial display and energy, *a word picture*.

The *foundations* must be built up (1) on cogent proofs, arguments.* (2) By *removing* false impressions and refuting groundless or anticipated objections.

§1. *Importance of the Proofs*

13. *Solidity* is indispensable for the speaker, and it is his duty to strive to attain it. Since eloquence is the champion of truth it ought to be founded on truth, on reasons, on principles, on facts; and no thoughtful audience will pay any attention to the speaker unless the latter be devoted entirely to the cause of truth.

* Some authors, as Kleutgen, give a more extended meaning to this idea and divide the argumenta into probantia, illustrantia, moventia, according as their aim is *to prove* to the intellect, *to delight* the æsthetic temperament, or to *move* the passions. Greek Rhetoricians distinguish ἐπιχειρήματα προτρεπτικά (προτροπή; *suasio*), also παθητικά in antithesis to ἀποδεικτικά, which principally appeal to the reasoning powers. We say *principally* because, though the παθητικά take effect by means of the influence which they exercise upon the heart, indirectly, they appeal also to the reason, for they incline the mind not only to recognize the true and the good as such, but at the same time to wish that it may be true and good. (On the προτροπή and ἀποτροπή cf. Arist. 1, 3 sq., Anaxim. (at the beginning) and Plato, Diog. Læert. sect. 59; in this work proofs and motives are often treated as being synonymous.

ELOQUENCE

The most tremendous efforts of eloquence, the most moving appeals, the liveliest illustrations, the most brilliant developments are feeble and as a rule ridiculous, unless they rest upon the solid foundation of truth. This must be held up before all and placed in such a light that reason, obstinate and perverted by prejudice as it frequently is, may be reduced to agreement and submission. As long as the reason remains unsatisfied, and while it struggles and makes objections, the way to the heart remains closed. Hence Cicero lays down absolutely, "Probare necessitatis est"* Aristotle: Αἱ γὰρ πίστεις ἔντεχνόν ἐστι μόνον. τὰ δ᾽ ἄλλα προσθῆκαι. "Proofs alone are essential;† the rest is supplementary."

Quintilian: "Cetera quæ continuo magis orationis tractu decurrunt, in auxilium atque ornamentum argumentorum comparantur, nervisque illis, quibus causa continetur, adiciunt superinducti corporis speciem."‡ Thus soundness is the soul of true eloquence; hence justly is it called by a French critic, *la raison passionée*.

The first care, then, of the speaker must be directed to this matter; the proposition which he wishes to develop in a successful manner should be looked upon as the very soul of his discourse; and with this unwavering aim, all other thoughts admitted and presented, only so far as they can help in giving

---

* Orat. 21, 69.

†1, 1, 3. That is *per se;* but since man is acted on by other than mere reasoning power, the προσθῆκαι are indispensable. See No. 32, "Means by which the Orator may Prevail"; No. 40, "Importance of the Emotions."

Aristotle, in the passage quoted, blames the rhetoricians of his time because they devoted too little attention to the oratorical proof, since it is the very pith of persuasion (σῶμα τῆς πίστεως) so far as the art of speaking is considered in itself. According to him the only really necessary materials of the art are the proofs (hence the term, πίστεις ἔντεχνοι), and so far is it only for him, δύναμις περὶ ἕκαστον τοῦ θεωρῆσαι τὸ ἐνδεχόμενον πιθανόν. All other elements which are called in rhetoric, *mores, affectus, elocutio, dispositio partium orationis* have nothing to do with the matter, but they are necessary on account of the audience, or they are an addition required by relative and external necessities, προσθῆκαι. He speaks very clearly on this subject in the first chapter of the Third Book. So far as the power of persuasion is essential to eloquence, ῥητορική is styled in Plato (Gorgias, 453) δημιουργὸς πειθοῦς.

‡ "But other efforts of oratory which run through the continued course of a speech are designed as aids or embellishments to the arguments, and give to the skeleton of the discourse the appearance of a living body."

to it, a luminous, strong and convincing energy. While we insist so forcibly on the quality of the proof, we confine ourselves to those things which stand in need of proof. For with regard to self-evident proofs or facts, the words of Quintilian hold true: "In rebus apertis argumenta tam sit stultum, quam in clarissimum solem mortale lumen inferre."* As the proof, so the refutation (which, after all, is only another kind of proof) must be perfectly convincing, and in the eyes of the audience absolutely triumphant. Feeble and imperfect answers do more harm than the objections themselves. To guard against faulty or tricky conclusions (sophisms) or to expose these in the course of the refutation, one should keep in mind that they take their origin from many different sources. It is a sophism (1) if a man proves something which was never in question, and so fights the air, neglecting the points at issue (*ignoratio elenchi*); or (2) if he assumes as proved what is still the question under debate, begging the question (*petitio principii*), so proving A by B, and B by A, and moving in a circle (*circulus vitiosus*); (3) by confusing, indiscriminately, cause and effect, ignorance and consequent non-existence, collective and distributive ideas; by starting from a false definition; by generalizing from a single instance, by imperfect enumeration of parts, when by the use of ambiguous expressions, or by dropping out middle terms of the argument (*saltus in demonstrando*), a mere appearance of proof is produced instead of a real proof.†

§2. *Sources of Proof. Introductory to the Topics.*

14. The most fertile source, and the one that can be replaced by no other, is a perfect knowledge of the subject under discussion and reflection upon it from all points of view; reflection, engaging not only the mind but the heart, for the heart is the seat of eloquence, not only inspiring the speaker with great passions, but even with great thoughts. "Les grandes pensées viennent du cœur," says Vauvenargues; and Quintilian: "Pectus est quod disertos facit."‡

*5, 12, 8. To argue in support of a matter that is clear is as foolish as to bring a lighted taper into the broad daylight.

†Aristotle treats of these points very clearly and briefly in his Rhet. 2, 24.

‡10, 17, 15.

ELOQUENCE

In the same sense an old author calls the sublime "the echo of the soul's greatness."

What Cicero says of the speaker's knowledge in general is peculiarly applicable to the knowledge which the latter should have of his own subject of discourse: "Ex rerum cognitione efflorescat et redundet oportet oratio; quæ nisi subest res ab oratore percepta et cognita, inanem quandam habet elocutionem et pæne puerilem."*

The speaker should try to seize upon the great and noble features of his subject, i.e., to conceive it in the *grandest way possible*. To succeed in this he must consider his subject in its chief moral or practical aspects, or make it the ally of some startling truth or fact, going deep into the nature of the subject, its origin, its consequences and the influence it exerts in various directions; or, again, he should study the great orators and observe how in their masterpieces they contrive to magnify the importance of the subjects they treat of, Demosthenes, for example (particularly in *De Corona*), Cicero, Chrysostom, Bossuet, Bourdaloue, Burke, O'Connell.

To enable the young speaker to think out his subject, teachers of eloquence have indicated certain headings and rules for his observance which may serve as points of departure. These categories, as they are called, commonplaces (*loci communes*, τόποι) may be looked upon as in some way the sources whence meditation may drink the fullness of its oratorical overflow. The name commonplaces, or rather platitudes, is also often applied to things in which mere talkativeness takes refuge for want of something better to say. It is self-evident that our *loci communes* have nothing in common with these. The pedantry with which the rhetorical topics were often treated gave occasion to the later rhetoricians to urge that their employment was without any practical bearing. We are not in agreement with this view, and we introduce here the most important elements of the *loci communes*

---

*De Orat. 1, 6, 20, or 1, 5, 20. Here the Roman orator is in closest agreement with Aristotle, according to whom the proofs and the cause should above all speak for themselves: Δίκαιον, αὐτοῖς ἀγωνίζεσθαι τοῖς πράγμασιν. Ὡς τε τἆλλα ἔξω τοῦ ἀποδεῖξαι, περίεργά ἐστιν.

for the *twofold reason of drawing attention to the manner in which great orators make use of them* and *of bringing together* under the eyes of the intending speaker the *most telling points of view under which a subject may be contemplated.* Cicero's judgement on the importance and application of the topics is entirely favourable, and we must give to the opinion and experience of the greatest orator of all times a consideration other than what we owe to the criticisms of many moderns, one-sided as these are, and sometimes not even the result of any practical experience.*

It may be said that mature reflection will suggest all the matter necessary to the speaker; but it is just mature reflection that is the most difficult thing for the young, and for that reason they must receive every help possible. Now the so-called commonplaces are only *the expression of the chief relations* in which the intellect of man stands with regard to the objects presented to his mind. Thus they are suggested by nature itself, they supply the mind with a *method* of *developing thought*; and this leads to meditation in the true sense. They cannot *take the place* of meditation as was maintained by some of the old sophists, but they can make it easy; they are not substitutes for the necessary knowledge but a help to its right use.

§ 3. *Topics of the Motives*

15. *The topics* (τοπική, τέχνη, Topica, loci) *are simply the catagories†used in working out and developing the argument of*

* De Orat. 2, 35, 147 sq.: "Cum ad inveniendum in dicendo tria sint"; 2, 30, 131: "Sed ii loci ei demum oratori prodesse possunt"; 2, 41, 174: "Ut enim si aurum cui, quod esset multifariam defossum." . . . closing with these words: "His igitur locis in mente et cogitatione defixis et in omni re ad dicendum posita excitatis, nil erit quod oratorem effugere possit non modo in forensibus disceptationibus, sed omnino in ullo genere dicendi."

Another writer (Broeckart) also remarks: "Those who reject these topics have no means of teaching how an idea should be developed or a proof worked out; and in their endeavours they become inconsistent, doing and teaching the very things they profess to blame."—Guide du jeune Littérateur, art. Top.

†*Categories:* "If we say anything about some object which has an existence of its own, we must speak either of its quantity (*quantitas*) or its qualities (*qualitas*) or its relation (*relatio*) to the things around it; what it is doing (*actio*) or what is being done to it (*passio*); of the place (*ubi*) or time (*quando*) of its existence,

a speech. Now, since the aim of all eloquence is to direct and determine the opinions of others, *arguments* must be based on *motives*, that is to say, they must be of such a nature that the course recommended by the orator secures the approval of his audience. Corresponding to the three main categories of motives, there are three aspects under which a suggested line of action may be considered beneficial; (1) it may be *good* (lawful, conformable to duty, noble, just, becoming); (2) it may be *pleasant*, or (3) *useful* (perhaps necessary or of service in attaining some other desirable object). The *first* category is made use of by the orator, who, in displaying the justice and sublimity of his cause, exhorts his hearers to a brave fight, or who warns his audience that sin is an offence against God's commands; he employs the *second* when he urges us to strive after heaven by describing the happiness of the elect, or in order to fill us with the fear of hell, puts before our eyes the awful punishment of the damned; when he recommends the reading of good books as a means of forming the mind, or, by putting before our eyes the evil results of reading bad ones, dissuades us from their perusal, he uses the *third* category.

Under certain circumstances still further advantage from the use of these categories may be derived by keeping before the mind considerations concerning (1) God, thankfulness, love, justice; (2) ourselves intrinsic and extrinsic, temporal and eternal good; (3) our neighbours, family, country, church, especially good or evil accruing to society, honour or dishonour.

Bishop Flavian employed these and similar arguments in his speech before the Emperor Theodosius, when endeavouring to obtain mercy for the inhabitants of Antioch. His masterly use of them gained his point.*

Demosthenes from the consideration of what honour and necessity demanded, and from consideration of the dangers,

or of its position (*situs*), or external belongings (*habitus*). These form the nine different classes under one or other of which every accident must fall, and these added to substance form the ten categories, as they are called by Aristotle, under which all ideas or concepts ultimately fall."—From *Manuals of Catholic Philos.*, Logic. Rich. F. Clarke, S.J.

* See Extract xxii.

shame and weakness of any other policy, shapes reasons for urging the Athenians to arm against Philip and his followers. The same motives we see urged by Cicero in the first half of *Pro Lege Manilia* (war against Mithridates) and in the seventh *Philippic* (reasons against peace with Anthony); also in the second part of his Defence of Milo (the ignominy and disgrace incurred by Rome had Clodius gained the day). Compare the peroration of this speech; other examples we find in the Catiline Orations.

St Gregory of Nazianzum, one of the most celebrated of Greek orators, has bequeathed to us a grand but short example* in his address to the Imperial Prefect on behalf of the inhabitants of the City.

§4. *Universal Topics. Sources of Information*

16. The topic just treated of by a natural sequence leads us to the Common or Universal one, formulated in the first place by Aristotle, and afterwards worked out by other rhetoricians. By its aid we are led to approach the subject in a methodical manner, to regard it from all points of view, and so to gain those complete and persuasive thoughts, by which the cause of the speaker is strengthened, and hence the good which he recommends, or the evil he deplores, is presented in its full light to the minds of the hearers, and exerts its influence on their will.

According to the ancients we distinguish two main sources of information, the *intrinsic* and the *extrinsic*.†

---

*I put Christ before you—His humiliation for our sake—His sorrows—His sufferings—His cross—His nails; The Blood of Christ—His Grave—His Resurrection—His Ascension . . . etc.

†The ancients, since Aristotle, have divided arguments into (1) ἔντεχνα, *artificialia*, due to art, which the speaker has been obliged to shape by reflection out of the subject *arte et ingenio*, these correspond to our intrinsic topics; (2) ἄτεχνα, *inartificilia, quæ foris accedunt* (witnesses, for example, documents), corresponding to our extrinsic loci.

Before the advent of Christianity, with its train of new ideas regarding the relations between God, man and the world at large, and the dissemination of these ideas by the printing press, there was more of art in the assiduous use of the topics; and we must always bear this in mind when we form a judgement on them.

Although they are principally intended for seeking and developing proofs, they are of use also in discovering and exploiting other resources, by which

ELOQUENCE

Article I. *Intrinsic Topics* (Loci, Sources).

17. We give here the most essential:

(1) Those which show what the subject is in *itself*: (a) definition; (b) genus and species; (c) enumeration of parts; (d) etymology.

(2) Those which show what the subject is in *relation* with *other* things: (a) cause; (b) effect; (c) circumstances; (d) antecedents and consequences.

(3) Those which show what the subject is in *contrast* with other things: (a) unlikeness; (b) likeness; (c) opposition.

The first and third of these classes are of service also in the *exposition** of a subject.

A. *Topics showing what the Subject is in itself*

(a) *Definition*

18. *The definition announces the nature of the subject*, and in many cases throws light at once on the good or evil in it; so, for example, the definition of God, religion, providence, justice, patriotism, charity, etc., supplies the orator with the most abundant material for portraying them; from the definition of truth follows the senselessness of pride, the degradation of hypocrisy; from the definition of fidelity, friendship or patriotism, the horror of treachery in any of its forms; from the definition of government, the evil of unrest and anarchy; from the definition of man and human dignity, the vileness of lust, slavery, etc.

There are two kinds of definitions; the *philosophical* and the *oratorical*.

The *philosophical* definition of a general idea consists in the declaration of its *distinguishing qualities*—the genus (*genus proximum*) and the species (*differentia specifica*); the *oratorical* is a *freer* and *larger-handed* way of dealing with a subject; a short description of it, according to its parts, its properties or its effects being given.

An example will make it clear. Cicero defines glory philosophically thus: "Gloria est frequens de aliquo fama cum

a subject may be viewed in all possible lights and brought home to imagination, to heart and will; they are particularly helpful in rhetorical development so we shall at once treat of them.   * See above, 12.

laude";* then oratorically: "Gloria est illustris ac pervagata magnorum, vel in suos cives, vel in patriam, vel in omne genus hominum, fama meritorum."†

To ensure a solid argument, it is not unfrequently necessary to start from the strictly philosophical definition; at the same time, not only is the oratorical definition often united with it, to impress on the mind and imagination of the audience by example and illustration what the philosophical definition supplies only in bare outline, but it sometimes supplants the latter and is more frequently employed, at least in addresses to the crowd. Meaningless words, mere chatter, must, however, be guarded against. Some examples may supply a clearer understanding of the use and development of the oratorical definition:

Cicero defines history oratorically thus: "Testis temporum, lux veritatis, vita memoriæ, magistra vitæ, nuntia vetustatis."‡ Philosophy: "O vitæ philosophia dux, O virtutis indagatrix expultrixque vitiorum,"§ and elsewhere: "Philosophia omnium mater artium, quid est aliud nisi, ut ait Plato, donum, ut ego, inventum deorum?"‖

Donoso Cortes defines Patriotism: "How! What! That patriotism! Such a one as that to be called a true patriot! No! No! Have you any conception what it is to be a real patriot? It is to love, it is to hate, it is to feel as loves, as hates, as feels, our country."¶

A subject is often illustrated by a series of negations and affirmations, showing what it is not, then what it is, or vice versa. As a rule, great speakers manage to ring the changes in their longer definitions, as also in descriptions, so as to avoid stiffness and monotony. Thus in the following passage Cicero describes the Roman people:

"Do you think a mere crowd of hirelings, the Roman people, who allow themselves to use violence against the authorities, who besiege the Senate, who daily wish for murder, fires, plundering, a rabble such as you yourself could not possibly collect together unless you shut up all the taverns; a people to whom you gave as leaders Lentidius,

---

*De Inv. 2, 55, 166.   † Pro Marc. 8,26.   ‡ De Orat. ii 9, 36.
§ Tusc. v, 2, 5.   ‖ 1, 26, 64.   ¶ Speech on the Affairs of Rome.

Lollius, Plaguleius, Sergius? Oh, a beautiful worthy picture of the Roman people, well suited to strike terror into kings, foreign nations and the farthest peoples of the earth; a horde composed of slaves, hirelings, criminals and beggars! The Roman people was seen in all its grandeur and majesty, that time on the Campus Martius, when even you were allowed to speak against the authority and the will of the Senate and of all Italy. Yes, that people is the Lord of Kings, the conqueror and ruler of all nations which you, O wicked man, did look upon on that glorious day when the heads of the State, the foremost in rank and in age, voted with full understanding, not about the safety of a citizen, but about that of the State; when men had arrived at the Campus, not from emptied taverns but from municipal towns."*

So Cicero, by developing the definition of Consul, proves that Piso was not Consul, though he wore the consular dress.†

Æschines‡ expands at some length the definition of a friend of the people, and contrasts this picture with the life of Demosthenes§ to suggest his contention that Demosthenes had done no services for the State. Compare with this passage the definition of the homo popularis in Cicero‖ (introduction) and the arguments used to show that Labienus, the accuser of Rabirius did not deserve that name.¶ A splendid example is also afforded by E. von Ketteler's *The Kingdom of God's Grace* (negative and positive, or false and true notion of the power of the State) in his *Freiheit, Autorität und Kirche.*

These examples demonstrate how the definition may be employed both for developing the proofs and for oratorical expansion.

(b) *Genus and Species*

19. *Genus and Species*, being correlative ideas, are mutually illuminative. From the *general* we pass to the *particular*, and again from the *particular* to the *general*. All the properties of the genus belong also to the species and individual, and

---

* Pro Domo sua, c. 33, 89.   † In Pison. 10, 23.   ‡ Κατὰ Κτησιφ.
§ From 168, etc., ἀλλὰ δημοτικός ἐστιν, ἐὰν μὲν τοίνυν . . .
‖ Or. 2 de Lege agr. 3, 7, etc.   ¶ Pro Rab. c. 4, 6.

consequently what is true of the species and individual, is true also of the genus; but what is contrary to the nature of the genus, may not be affirmed of the species and individual. Since the great universal ideas offer the finest and the noblest field for the display of oratory, and so prepare the way for the most moving effects, we find that the greatest speakers make frequent use of this device of arguing *a genere*.

Cicero* enlarging (*a genere*) on the atrocity of parricide shows that Roscius, who is accused of this crime, is quite incapable of it; in *Pro Archia* he draws out at some length the qualities of a liberal education and the charm of a beautiful literature, and from this argues for the recognition which is due to the talents of a man like Archias; in his defence of Murena he maintains that the latter could not have assailed the plaintiff, Cato the Stoic, owing to the exaggerations and dissensions, excesses and differences which existed in the stoic schools; in the *pro Milone* he develops the proposition that cases occur in which a private individual may repel violence by the use of weapons, and concludes from this that Milo, even if Clodius has fallen at his hands, is not at once to be denounced as a law breaker.

Æschines attempts to prove that the offer of a crown by Ctesiphon to Demosthenes is against the laws. He introduces his subject with the general statement that all laws must be held sacred, whence follows the conclusion that the one specially directed against Demosthenes should also be kept inviolate. This device gives the stamp of dignity to his exordium.

Sonnenfels begins his panegyric on Maria Theresa with a general statement on royal birthdays, and thence makes the transition to the birthday of Maria Theresa: "The birth of a future sovereign is the most doubtful of all presents that heaven can bestow on a people. Either their happiness is secured to them by his goodness or the lamentable gift of the Creator of mankind is a most terrible scourge to his own kingdom and to those of others. It is a tragic necessity when a weeping people is forced to celebrate with

* Pro Roscio Amer.

magnificence of pomp the day they execrate in secret, a day which they would wish could be wiped out from the annals of time, or had never been. But what unspeakable joy there is in celebrating a day which gave them an upright, a good, a wise ruler, a friend of mankind, a father; a day blest of a people full of the joy of gratitude!"

When is a subject to be proposed in a universal or generic form, when in its species? A few points may be suggested.

(1) When a speaker is confronted with a trivial theme or one that has little interest, he may then refer it to some higher principle with which it is connected, in other words, draw out his discourse *a genere*. Only when the speaker ventures beyond the narrow limits of his theme without, however, losing himself; when he expands his thoughts and rises to a point from which the subject is viewed not only in its full contour but also in its bearings on the most absorbing interests of mankind; then only does the orator move, and grasp and convulse his hearers.*

Here, however, care is to be taken (1) not to wander too *far afield;* (2) not to employ the generic expansion for every trifling subject but only for those ideas which are capable of *an elevated treatment;* (3) to *throw real light* on the subject and not to press the latter into the background or to sink it altogether.†

Finally, (4) the generic development should not act wholly in, or even ostentatiously invade the domain of pure proof, so as to convey a feeling of want of colour and form, or of taking refuge in abstractions, but it ought to come down to the concrete, the actual, the living (history, narrative, etc.), and in the development to illustrate the universal by the particular. This is all the more possible since the universal always presents itself under definite forms and in individuals.

There is always a danger in the use of the generic development of falling into abstractions or generalities. One

---

* Crevier, Rhétorique, p. 1. In Bossuet and Bourdaloue their peculiar elevation is often due to this translation of the subject to a more universal plane.

† This was a misuse peculiar to the Declamatives or Sophists among the ancients, and not unfrequently the pleaders at the bar were guilty of it by labouring among vague generalities or mere commonplaces instead of attending to their case and proving the point at issue.

example of it may be seen in Engel's panegyric on Frederick II, where the whole of the first part of the address is occupied with the idea of a king in general, and becomes more or less of a moral philosophical essay, while it is only in the shorter second portion that the real theme is broached. The generic development requires always a becoming brevity.

(2) If, on the other hand, the matter is *universal*, it is admissible to change the universal proposition to a specific one, because as such it makes a deeper impression than the general one; at the same time it simplifies it by giving it a more practical character. Hence it is more likely to produce the definite effect contemplated by the speaker. This remark has a peculiar application to pulpit oratory, whereof more in its own place.

(c) *Division or Enumeration of Parts*

20. The breaking-up of an idea into several subordinate ideas, or the division of a whole into its parts is a familiar proceeding on the part of the speaker, for thereby his subject gains in clearness and the real wealth of striking thoughts and proofs which it contains are exploited.

Application. (1) For the division of the theme or the subdivision of its chief heads see below under the heading *Arrangement*.

(2) For the development of the proofs, the parts are considered in relation to the whole, whether it is required to prove from the united existence of all parts the existence of the whole, or from the absence of one or several parts the non-existence of the whole. Of course, the whole may be considered in relation to the parts; for where the whole exists naturally there must be the parts. In the disjunctive treatment either one member is negatived and the others disjunctively affirmed, or one is affirmed and the others in a body denied.

Cicero proved by enumeration of parts that the roll of commander-in-chief belonged to Pompey in the most supreme degree: "Ego enim sic existimo in summo imperatore quattuor has res inesse oportere, scientiam rei militaris, virtutem, auctoritatem, felicitatem." Then he shows that these qualities are combined in the highest measure in Pompey: "Quis hoc homine scientior unquam aut fuit aut esse debuit?" Thence he draws the conclusion that Pompey is the man for the time and ought to be placed in command of the Asiatic forces.*

As an example of disjunctive treatment the invective against Verres† will serve when Cicero attacks him in the following argument about the theft perpetrated on Hejus: either (a) Hejus gave the images of his own free will; or (b) because he was induced by the large sums of money offered; or (c) under pressure of adverse circumstances: "If these motives are not to be discovered, then it is plain you took them from him; for neither the first, nor the second, nor the third motive can be maintained; hence only the last is the true one. I, therefore, affirm that Hejus was induced neither by any sudden desire, nor by any sudden necessity, nor by the large amount of money offered to sell these statues, but that you took them from him."‡

(3) In the case of oratorical *amplification* and *description*, division lends to the subject a singular vividness and makes it specially interesting by individualization: a glimpse of a real being, shown in all the various moods of its character, has much more fascination for a hearer than a mere generality. Division likewise gives more weight to an idea because its various aspects are prominently displayed.

Cicero, instead of saying, "All hate thee, O Piso," puts it: "The *senate* hates thee—and according to thy own confession, justly—as the enemy and destroyer of its dignity and power; nay, even of its very rank and name. The *equestrian order* cannot bear the sight of thee, because during thy consulship, Lucius Ælius, one of its most famous and respected members, was banished. The *Roman people* desires thy condemnation. *The whole of Italy* curses thee, because thou didst treat with contempt its orders and commands."

Similar to this is the following passage against the same

* Pro Lege Man. 10-16, 49. † De Signis, c. 6-8.

‡ Similarly *Pro Rabirio* (c. vii). In the nature of things he must have adopted one of these three lines of conduct: he must either have been with Saturnius, or with the good men, or he must have been lying abed: to be with Saturnius was an act of insanity and wickedness. Virtue and honour and shame compelled him to range himself on the side of the Consuls.

Piso on the matter of his disgraceful government of his Consular province:

"Is there any single undertaking or achievement of yours in that province on which you could have congratulated yourself in reporting it to the Senate? Recall the way in which Macedonia was harassed, the disgrace of losing the towns, the plundering of the allies, the despoiling of the lands, the fortifying of Thessalonica, the occupation of a military road, the destruction of our army by sword and famine, by cold and pestilence."*

The following example combines division and its development by opposites. "One man drinks turbid water trickling from the holes of a cistern; another from the inexhaustible source of a fresh spring—which of the two will quench his thirst more thoroughly? Such is the difference between the sensual pleasures of this world and the sublime joys of the Holy Spirit. What are the pleasures offered by the world? Are they those of eating and drinking, which engender disgust and nausea after but a short indulgence in them? Are they riches and luxury? But these are a source of anxiety and care, nor can they accompany us beyond the grave. Is it honour such as the world gives? This is often deceitful and vanishes like smoke Is it the satisfaction of pleasure and lust? Yet these destroy both body and soul. Such are the sensuous, evil and fleeting pleasures of the world, turbid as the water in an unclean cistern."†

Care must be taken in the use of these topics not to enumerate trivial things or those foreign to the matter in hand, and, especially, must the orator be on his guard against prolixity. The various points must follow each other in a definite order, so as to form one connected whole, and thus fix themselves in the hearer's mind. An irregular, confused array of matter is difficult to memorize. The best division is when the order is arranged so as to form a climax.

(d) *Etymology*

21. The etymology of a proper name or of any term may

---

*Cf. also Pro Lege Mar. c. 11; Post Red. ad Qu. 1; 2 Cat. 4, 7.
† Rive, 2nd Whitsun Sermon.

suggest thoughts which can be developed with advantage, e.g., "Si consul est, qui patriæ consulit, quid aliud fecit Opimius?"*

Few opportunities present themselves for the employment of this device, which rather lends itself to pedantry, trifling or vulgarity. Still there are occasions in which it may do excellent service in bringing to the surface a beautiful meaning, or a happy illustration (such as may occur in occasional speeches). Certain terms have a profound meaning of their own as *Pius*, *Augustus*, *senatus*, *philosophus;* while others have it by their applicability to one or another personage. The emphasizing of certain names or titles (by special reference to their meaning) is an especially efficacious means of giving a rebuke; thus in Scipio's speech to his mutinous troops:

"Never should I have believed that in the presence of my soldiers words would fail me. . . . But how I am to address you, I really know not: thought and speech fail me; I do not even know what I should call you. *Citizens?* you who have denied your country? *soldiers?* you who have scorned your commander and broken your military oath? *enemies?* Truly in your faces, your bodies, your clothing, your manner, I recognize my fellow-citizens; but in your deeds, your speeches, your plans—*enemies.*" †

Not quite in good taste is the use which Cicero makes of the name of Verres (*Verres* meaning "Boar" and *verrere* "to sweep out"). "Oh! the glorious feast of Verres! Tell me where you have been and not carried the celebration of it with you? What house, what town have you entered, nay even what temple without leaving it swept and cleared out?"

In the pulpit this method is of special application, because certain Scriptural names were settled by God himself, e.g., Jesus, Peter, Abraham, etc. So we find in the fathers of the Church the beautiful definition, "Christianus, alter Christus," in *St Bernard* a happy passage on the name of the martyr St Victor‡ the beautiful discourses on the names of Jesus and Mary.§

* De Orat. 2, 39, 165.　　† Livy, 28, 27.　　‡ Serm. 2 de S. Victore.
§ Serm. 2 de Circumcis. and Hom. 15 in Cant.; Hom. 2 super Missus est and in Nativ. B.V.

RHETORICAL AIDS

(a) *Causes*

22. Under the name of cause comes everything that conditions the being of another thing. Like the philosopher, the speaker considers a subject (a) according to its material cause; (b) according to the final cause, or the end and limitations; (c) according to the formal cause, that is the idea of a place or of some thing. In a house, for instance, the efficient cause is the person who constructs the building or has it built; the final cause the use to which the house is destined, as dwelling, school, etc.; the formal cause the plan according to which it is built.*

Cause and effect are so intimately united that the speaker finds no difficulty in arguing from the existence and the properties of the cause to those of its effect, and vice versa. In this connexion two points are to be observed: (1) that the relation between cause and effect really exists; when the connexion between the results of an observation and what is considered to be its cause is not indubitable, it ought to be proved; (2) that a distinction should be made between one cause and another, i.e., between free causes, moral causes, necessary causes. In the last-mentioned instance there exists a necessary, unchangeable proportion between cause and effect; not so in the others which may have various results, so that they can be argued from only with limitations. From the proposition, for instance, that all men owe their origin to the same Creator, it does not follow that all men are alike. So, too, the conclusion would be false in this reasoning: the author of creation is eternal, therefore also the created are eternal. The speaker must in every case not only establish the relation between cause and effect, but also show how and in what special way. In their rhetorical use, causes are often employed as motives appealing to the will, then as proofs for the intellect, and often too they serve as divisions of a speech. According to circumstances the opposite of the

---

* The material and formal cause of the metaphysician is of little practical use to the orator.

23

causes, or the hindrances, are often brought into review; this is a device to be seen in Demosthenes' *Philippics*.

The development of causes is a very marked element in the political speeches of Demosthenes, as in all sound eloquence, and any one of his speeches illustrates the use of this topic in its general as in its particular aspects. Of exceptional note is the passage in the *De Corona* where Demosthenes develops the reason why he and not Æschines was called upon by the people to speak the panegyric over those who had fallen in defence of their country. πολλὰ καὶ καλὰ καὶ μεγάλα ἡ πόλις, Αἰσχίνη, καὶ προείλετο καὶ κατώρθωσε δι' ἐμοῦ.*

In the second speech against Rullus,† Cicero reveals to the Roman people the grounds on which the decemvirs were pressing the partition of the Campanian lands: "Num obscure regnum constituitur?" In *Pro lege Manilia* he demonstrates the perils of the Asiatic campaign from the strength and energy of those who are leagued together against Rome. In similar wise he shows the innocence of Milo and the guilt of Clodius: "How then are we to prove that Clodius laid a plot against Milo? It is quite sufficient in the case of such a wicked, of such an audacious monster, to prove that he had great reason for doing so: he had great hopes founded on Milo's death; it would have been of the greatest service to him. Hence, Cassian's test—who is the gainer?—applies in this case. For although good men cannot be induced to commit crimes by any advantage whatever, wicked men can be induced by very trifling ones. Now if Milo were slain, Clodius stood to gain. For not only would he be prætor without having as consul one who would never countenance any of his crimes; but also he would have those men for consuls who, if they did not aid him, would at all events connive at all his proceedings."‡

(b) *Effects*

23. Effects give better opportunities to the speaker, especi-

---

* 285-8 cf. further 2 Olynth. 6, 23 ; 3 Olynth. 30 sqq.

† De Leg. agr. 2, 28, 75.

‡ Pro. Mil. 12, 32. Cf. also Pro Roscio Amer. 30, 84. In this speech he shows that the plaintiff has no reason to continue his accusation since he has already acquired everything which could give a spur to the accusation, " Prædia mea tu possides," etc.

ally to the platform speaker, than causes, since they are more fully appreciated, and lend themselves more easily to illustration. They are employed:

(1) *In the proof*, since they bear the same relation to the causes as the fruit to the tree, so too in the motives, they determine the will for or against a given procedure. Like the causes the effects and consequences may be used to mark:

(2) *The divisions of a discourse.* Thus Ciceri divides his discourse on an evil conscience: (a) the evil conscience prevents the sinner enjoying the sweets of this life; (b) causes him in addition to suffer the pains of the next.

(3) Finally, in conjunction with division, they help to *illustrate* and *expand the subject.* In dealing with facts the speaker will ordinarily develop the effects in their historical sequence, or he will group them according to the laws of climax, proceeding from the smaller to the greater, as in moral subjects, e.g., the effects of avarice.

Demosthenes proves, from the effects following upon his eloquence and his policy, its honourable character, and inveighs against Æschines with the additional argument, that the latter's conduct of affairs never had any successful issue. The principal passage to which at present we can only give a reference, is in the *De Corona*, 297-306: ταύτης τοίνυν τῆς οὕτως αἰσχρᾶς καὶ περιβοήτου συστάσεως. . . .

Cicero demonstrates in a similar manner that Antony is an enemy to the State. "Just as in the seed lies the germ of trees and plants, so in you was the germ of this piteous war.* You complain that these armies of the Roman people have been destroyed? Antony has destroyed them. Many famous citizens are missing? Antony has torn them away from you. The prestige of the Senate is lowered? Antony has lowered it. Indeed all that we have since gone through—and what misery have we not experienced?—all we have to thank— to give every one his due—Antony for, and him only."†

Colmar begins his sermon on bad books with a brief description of the pernicious effects of such literature.

* Civil war by Cæsar.

† 2 Phil. 22, 55. Cf. also Pro Lege Manil. xvii, 52; xix, 57, in which Cicero by referring to the effects of the Lex Gabinia justifies the Lex Manilia.— Pro Archia, vii, 16.

Mallinckrodt says of the effects of the struggle against the Church: "You know not the effects of Christian conviction. Sorrow begets willingness to suffer, and when you behold our shepherds in prison or in banishment, do you think there is any lack of willingness to expose themselves even to this fate? And if our priests have followed and continue to follow this example, the laity will not fail either, and the desired effects, gentlemen, will not be produced by banishment! You will have to look for still sharper weapons; what weapons will you employ when we, in the midst of all, think only of the words *Per crucem ad lucem—Through the cross to light.*"

Nirschl proves the existence and the attributes of God from the consideration of the universe. "When the universe is considered, and the countless animate and inanimate beings therein, the question is unconsciously asked: who has called all these things into being? who sustains them? why are they here? who has produced this world, this sublime work of art, which reveals such immense power, such profound wisdom; what is its object? Numberless stars move in their appointed orbit in the heavens, whole flocks of birds fly through the air filling it with their joyful sounds, thousands of animals roam over the land, millions of flowers adorn the pastures, the waters team with life, even in a small drop, a whole world of activity is concealed! Who has given being to all? who preserves them? why have they been created? At the contemplation of all this, the astonished and thoughtful mind asks itself these questions. How does it answer them? how does it solve them? It sees in the world the revelation of a power without bounds, Wisdom, Goodness and Beauty, and recognizes therein the existence of an everlasting, almighty, all-wise, all-good and all-beautiful divine being."*

(c) *Circumstances*

24. Careful observation of the various circumstances which give character to a subject, or which in any way accompany it, accentuate its importance, and show it under varying

---

* Necessity of the Christian Religion. See also Speech on the Christian Faith, by Mr Chauncey Depew.

lights, ought to be cultivated by the speaker, since it furnishes him by turns with almost the whole of his matter, the grounds and motives to be developed, and in most cases supplies the point of view which he is to adopt in each case in turn. The clever manipulation of circumstances is the characteristic mark of the speaker as it is of the general.

There are various kinds of circumstances: some related to *persons*, *things*, *place* and *time;* others, which make a matter *easy*, *praiseworthy*, *useful*, *necessary* or, on the contrary *difficult*, *blameworthy*, *useless*, *impossible;* others, which *aggravate* or *extenuate*, etc.

The different points of view under which a subject may be contemplated have been expressed in the following verse:

> Quis? quid? quibus auxiliis? cur? quomodo? quando?
> or: Quid? quis? ubi? per quos? quoties? cur? quomodo? quando?

Examples. The first we find in Livy. When Horatius gained his victory in the combat with the Curiatii, his sister, who had been espoused to one of them, reproached him bitterly for his triumph. Horatius, carried away by his fury, killed her on the spot. He was cited before the court and condemned to death. From this sentence he appealed to the people. His own father came forward to plead for him. It may be seen how striking, how powerful in its appeal to the popular mind by virtue of their picturesqueness are the circumstances of time and place. After embracing his son, the father pointed to the arms of the Curiatii, which were hanging there, and then began to speak: "Romans," said he, "can you bear to see bound beneath a gallows amidst scourges and tortures, him whom you just now beheld marching and decorated with spoils, and exulting in victory? a sight so shocking that even the eyes of the Albani could not endure it. Go, lictor, bind those hands, which but a little time ago, with arms, gained sovereignty for the Roman people! Go, cover the head of the liberator of this city; hang him on the gallows; scourge him either within or without the pomœrium, so it be only amid those javelins and spoils of the enemy; or without the pomœrium, only amid the graves of the Curiatii! For whither can you bring this

youth, where his own glories will not redeem him from the
ignominy of punishment?"

Compare also the speech of Pacuvius to Perolla* to be
cited later, the short address of Vectius Messius to the
Volsci surrounded by the Romans;† Hannibal's speech to
his troops.‡ "On right hand and left two seas shut us in. We
possess no ship in which we can escape. Before us is the
Po, a stream greater and swifter than the Rhone; at our
back is the Alps, which you found difficulty in crossing in
full health and strength. There is nothing for it, soldiers,
but to conquer or die!"

Cicero, relating the circumstances of Clodius's meeting
with Milo, uses them with great dexterity to clear the latter
of the charge brought against him.§

In popular oratory this topic can be used with tremendous
effect. O'Connell in his Edinburgh speech introduces an
opportune reference to the scenery amidst which he is speaking: "When I look around me and encounter in the faces
of this immense assembly the expression of most perfect
well-being; when I embrace in the same glance the beautiful panorama which lies extended before me; oh, then, with
the contemplation of such an entrancing picture, and with
that sacred love which I have always felt for nature, my
soul seems bowed down under the weight of most rapturous
feeling, and from the depths of my heart the cry goes out,
What man would be such a coward as not to fight with joy
for so noble a country?"

(d) *Antecedents and Consequences*

25. *Antecedentia, consequentia,* i.e., things preceding or
following upon an event,‖ without, however, the circumstances being always identical with cause or effect. The speaker
has to dwell at one time, in the past, at another time, in the

---

* 23, 9.   † 4, 23.   ‡ 21, 43.

§ Pro Mil. 20, 54. The circumstances of the place are dealt with in 20, 53
See further De Supplicio., 37.

‖ According to Cicero, different from the preceding categories, because the
adjunEta are not necessarily connected with the circumstance, as the *antecedentia* and the *consequentia.* Cf. Cic., Top. 12, 53. Others consider these as
particular classes of the *adjuncta,* not separated from them.

future, to recount earlier or perhaps later phases of a situation, to make a truth or a proposal appear in its proper light, to clear up doubts, to show the change of events, in short, to represent his subject all rounded in its completeness or as necessity requires in its majesty.*

Besides its application by way of illustration and proof this topic can be well employed in rousing the emotions, especially rivalry, shame, hope and fear.† The caution to be observed here is to refrain from being too far fetched or pushing conclusions further than they will go.

Application of this topic. Cæsar proves that the charge of dancing made against Murena cannot be maintained since no one is in a condition to show that the accused ever indulged such laxity in morals as would naturally precede such an exhibition. In a similar way in his speech *Pro Roscio Amerino*‡ he refutes the charge of parricide and discovers a proof for Milo's innocence in the circumstance that in the latter's behaviour after the death of Clodius there was no sign of an evil conscience.§

Demosthenes shows from Philip's conduct before the war that he is not to be trusted, however he may proclaim his love of peace, e.g., in the remarkable passage of the second Philippic (20, 25) where he recounts the terms offered to the Messenianians and Argives: Πῶς γὰρ οἴεσθ, ἔφην, ὦ ἄνδρες Μεσσήνιοι; so too on the happenings in Chersonesus, 59.‖ In reminding the Athenians of the past glory of their city he suggests to them the strongest motives to inflame them with the desire of imitating the noble and disinterested patriotism of their forefathers.¶

C. Topics showing the Relation of the Subject by Comparison with other things

(a) Proper or logical Comparison

26. In order to gain a truer knowledge and understand-

---

* This glance that took in the scheme of things was often in Bossuet's hands an occasion for creating the most elevated and touching impressions, as may be seen in his funeral sermons and his discourses on the history of the world.

† See under Passions: Practical Application, no. 48.

‡ 13, 37; see below, no. 77.   § Pro Mil. c. 23, 24, cf. also 3 Cat. 5, 13.

‖ See below no. 55.   ¶ See especially the Third Olynthiac, 24, 26.

ing of a subject, it is usual to compare it with others. The orator also employs this method in what is called *logical comparison*. One truth that is to be proved is contrasted with another, in order to convince the hearer that the one is deserving of equal or greater importance than the other. If equality be claimed, we have the argumentum *a pari;* if superiority, in negative propositions, the argumentum *a majori ad minus,* in positive ones the *argumentum a minori ad majus.*

A pari. (Conclusion: "If . . . , so in like manner . . . ."): "I cannot understand, however, why thou spurnest me. Because I defend him whom thou accusest. But do not I also spurn thee, who accusest him whom I defend? Thou sayest: I accuse my enemy; and I defend my friend."*

A majori. (Conclusion: "If . . . , how much less . . . ?"

"If within the memory of man only few people have been found who, for the sake of their country, have offered themselves, without any prospect or hope of reward, to the swords of the enemy, can you, then, believe that anyone for the sake of a foreign country would run into danger, not merely without any prospect or reward, but also at the command of such a one?"†

A minori. (Conclusion: "If . . . . so much the more?")

"If our country binds us, and it really exercises so great a power over us that that very wise man‡ preferred his Ithaca, a tiny nest on steep rocks, to immortality, what love must not burst forth from us for that country, that amongst all lands, is the dwelling of virtue, bravery, power and dignity?"§ "If we defend ourselves as soon as a thief enters the house, if it is a disgrace to fold our arms as soon as an enemy

---

*Pro Sulla, 17, 48; cf. also 3 Cat. 1, 2: "Profecto quoniam . . ."; Phil. 5, 9, 25. "Ergo Hannibal hostis . . . ." Particularly the fine passage De Suppl. 64, 166: "Si tu apud Persas." See below, No. 29, Argum. ad hominem.

†Cic. Pro Ballo, 10, 26. So, too, Pro Domo suo, e. 41; Demost. 20 Cynth. 23: Οὐκ ἔνι. Here also belongs the saying of Terence: "Quem feret, si parentem non fert suum?"

‡Oddysseus: Calypso had promised him immortality, if he would remain on her island.

§De Orat. 1, 44, 196, cf. De Suppl. c. 58. Pro Balbo, c. 23; 54, "An lingua"; Pro Archia poet. c. 8: "Quis nostrum"; c. 9, "Ergo illi"; De suppl. 58, 149.

invades our country and hearths, how much more disgraceful it is that now so many hands are idle when all the great gifts of manhood are in question?"

Comparison is, like everything which appeals to the imagination, very important in popular oratory, and therefore much used. Hence Cicero forces the Roman people by means of continual comparisons to the determination that the war against Mithridates must be continued.

Compare also the vigorous passage of Demosthenes in his speech on the freedom of the inhabitants of Rhodes: "Would it not be disgraceful, O my countryman, that in those very circumstances when the Argives did not cower before the power and might of Lacedemon, you, you Athenians should cower before a person of barbarian origin and a woman too?* At least they could have pleaded that they had often been worsted in fight by the Lacedemonians, while, on the contrary, you have often overcome the king, and never suffered defeat at his hands or at those of his servants." †

Comparison appears though rather freely in the following example: "Have we not seen all that is beautiful in the reawakening of nature in spring—in the blooming of the flowers, in the charm of fruitful landscapes and romantic neighbourhoods! How often has the brilliancy of the starry heavens enchanted us! and which of the works of human skill have we not admired, in the capitals of mighty peoples, in the palaces of kings, in the museums with their treasures? And all this is nothing in comparison with the glory of heaven; *for no eye has ever seen it.* What have we not heard of the riches, pleasures, joys and happiness of the great and mighty of the earth! What does history recount to us of the treasures of Solomon and all his glory, of the riches of Crœsus, of the magnificence of the old Roman Empire, and of the luxury of the East! All that is but an empty shadow in comparison with the glory of Heaven! *For no ear has ever heard it.* Let us finally give free rein to our reason and imagination, let us unite everything we know about beauty, happi-

* Artemisia, Queen of Caria.   † 23.

ELOQUENCE

ness, honour, might and splendour, let us multiply it in such
measure as the powers of our mind allow, yet shall we *never*
get an idea of the reality of Heaven: *for never hath it entered
into the heart of man. . . ."*

(b) *Analogy and Comparison*

27. The similarity of two objects depends upon analogy
and comparison. The *former* is used to supply *proofs;* the
latter, *explanations*. Comparisons should not be pushed
further than is demanded by the needs of the orator.
Examples. From the analogy between the human body
and that of the state, Menenius Agrippa demonstrated the
necessity of unity amongst the citizens.† C. v. Ketteler says:
"It is impossible to dig up and destroy the foundation of
a house, to let it hang in the air, and still continue comforta-
bly living in it. Neither can we destroy the order of the universe without at last being enveloped in its ruins. If there
is no supernatural order, then truth is a riddle, law and
justice a riddle, and every man himself a riddle."‡

Demosthenes contrasts very powerfully the attitude of the
Athenians toward Philip, with the behaviour of an inexpe-
rienced boxer. "Your war with Philip differs in no respect
from the boxing of barbarians. For among them the party
struck always feels for the blow; strike him somewhere
else, there go his hands again; ward or look you in the face
he cannot or will not. So you, if you hear of Philip in the
Chersonese, vote to send relief there, if at Thermopylæ the
same; if anyone else, you run after his heels up and down,
and are commanded by him; no plan have you devised
for the war, no circumstance do you see beforehand, only
when you learn that something is done or about to be
done."§

He addresses Æschines, who accused him of having given
bad advice to his country: "What advantage has your eloquence been to your country? Now do you speak to us
about the past? It is as if a physician should visit his
patients, and not order or prescribe anything to cure the

* Rive, Sermon on the Ascension. † Liv. 2, 32.
‡ Freiheit, Autorität und Kirche, xiii. § Demosthenes, 1 Phil. 40.

32

disease, but on the death of one of them, when the last ceremonies were being performed, should follow him to the grave and expound how, if the poor fellow had done this or that, he would never have died. Idiot! Do you speak now?"*

(c) *Opposites and Dissimilitudes*

28. The dissimilarity as well as the similarity of things opens up a rich source of topics to the orator. The so-called *argumentum a contrario* and *a dissimili* and oratorical *contrast* are based upon dissimilarity. The former is used to corroborate, the latter aims, like similitude, at a *sharper definition of* and hence at a deeper consideration of the object.

(1) *Contrast* is to Eloquence what shading is to pictures. For example, in order to show the value of virtue the orator may picture the hatefulness of vice.

Beer contrasts in this way the advantages of peace with the fatal effects of discord: "What priceless treasure, real patriotism and love of peace offers can be best understood by recalling the stormy years when the torch of discord inflamed one nation against another, when the horrors of war shook the thrones of kings and the huts of the lowly; when no sound was heard save wails and curses; when man raged against man and blood flowed in streams; when neither goods nor property, neither honour nor life were safe; when religion, arts and sciences were in mourning; when from altars the prayers for mercy went up in vain to the Father in heaven. True, the heart of our beloved country was free from that scourge, but the blows which fell upon the confines of our own land and on other countries, reverberated in our midst like a shock of earthquake; we were witnesses of the inhuman cruelty and sorrows of many thousands who, in our country and capital sought and found the last consolation of being permitted to die among Christ's poor. Need we go back further to learn the horrors of war and

---

* De Corona; Demosth. de 242. Further examples see Cicero, Pro Roscio Comoedo 176, : "Ut ignis in aquam conjectus . . ."; Pro Sestio, 20, 45: "Etenim si mihi in aliqua . . ."; Pro Cluentio, 49, 138 : "Ut mare, quo sua natura tranquillum"; 4 Cat. 6, 12 : "Etenim quæro si quis paterfamilias."

the blessings of peace? Are not our hearts and our ears daily assailed by the news of the most sanguinary battles on the borders of Europe? Is not the gentle spirit of our religion in many a Christian country being forced to bend the knee to the idol of discord?"*

(2) This topic may appear in the course of the argument under three different forms:

(a) *When one statement being affirmed, another is denied;* as, Roscius loved his father, therefore he is not his murderer. This method is applicable to all sorts of contrasts.

The whole discourse *de Suppliciis* rests on the following argument: Verres in the government of the province entrusted to him showed himself to be avaricious, negligent, cruel; therefore, he was not, as Hortensius maintains, a distinguished leader in the field.

(b) *When one statement being denied, another is affirmed.* Here the rules of logic ought to be strictly observed—the distinction between contradictories and contraries;† thus, "He is not idle, therefore he is energetic"; but not "Roscius is not the murderer of his father, therefore he loves him."

(c) *When a conclusion* is drawn from the opposed natures of two things, as, for example, from opposite effects, causes, qualities, etc.‡ Thus Cicero concludes: "Quid! quam fatentur satis magnam vim esse in vitiis ad miseram vitam; nonne fatendum est eandem vim in virtute esse ad vitam heatam? Contrariorum enim contraria sunt consequentia."§ Further: "Si barbarorum est in diem vivere, nostra consilia sempiternum tempus spectare debent. Si Gracchus nefarie, præclare Opimius." ‖

From the different behaviour of heathens and Christians under accusation, Tertullian decisively proves the innocence of the Christians. "Those who have been induced

---

Erbaulicher Reden an Academiker, 5 Rede.

† *Propositions* are said to be *contrary* when one states more than is necessary to establish the other; *contradictory*, when one is exactly the opposite of the other. "He is poor, he is not poor" are contradictories; but—"He is poor, he is rich," are contraries.

‡ Locus ex dissimilitudine.   § Tusc. 5, 17.

‖ De Orat. 2, 40, 169. The famous consul and embittered opponent of G. Gracchus.

to commit a really great crime dare not even defend it as good. Every wicked action naturally covers us with fear and shame. Evil-doers, for example, always want to remain concealed; they avoid the public eye; they tremble when apprehended; deny when accused; do not even confess truthfully under torture; grieve when they are condemned; blame the attacks of the evil one upon them, or ascribe their deeds to fate or the stars. Now as to the Christian? No shame or grief has he, except that he did not believe before. When arrested, he rejoices. When interrogated, he does not defend himself, but of his own accord he confesses; when condemned, he gives thanks. What can be evil when the natural signs, fear, shame, denial, repentance and grief are lacking? Can there be any wrong in that over which the accused rejoices, where arrest is his desire and condemnation his happiness?"*

The incompatibility of certain things gives rise to the so-called Proof *ex absurdo* (also called *a repugnantibus*) because the truth of a statement is demonstrated from the conclusion to which the adoption of the opposite assumption would lead. This proof is often of very great strength, and is sometimes used in the corroboration (*confirmatio*), sometimes in the refutation.

By its use Lally-Tollendal (†) rebuts the charge made against him that in the defence of his father he was acting as spokesman and leader of the party opposed to the law.

"I, a time-serving tool! No! Never will I be tool of a faction of any faction on earth! I believe that in this matter my life hitherto will raise me above all suspicion." "I, head of a

---

* Apolog. c. 1.

† The speaker's father, Thomas Arthur, Comte de L. Tollendal, had been in command of the French troops in the East Indies. Through want of proper support he surrendered to the English, and for this his numerous personal enemies succeeded in getting him executed in 1766. His son, Trophimus Gerhard de Lally-Tollendal, the famous orator (b. 1751; d. 1830), undertook the vindication of his father's honour, and insisted on the withdrawal of the sentence, and by his eloquence had almost gained his point when a new opponent, Duval d'Epresmenil, set himself in opposition. The latter, a nephew of the most prominent of the unhappy general's accusers, maintained that by the wording of the revision proposed by Lally (he desired that on the heels of the cassation of the condemnation should follow an express and formal de-

party! that is an accusation I should never have expected.
The idea! I head a party! I, a lonely being, from my cradle
the victim of misfortune, from earliest childhood an orphan,
born of foreign parents.* I had hardly crossed the threshold
of my new home when I saw it reddened with the blood of my
family, the only one of my name, without connexion, without influence, without power. How now? Who are these
abject malcontents who could find their gain in rallying
around a madman and sharing the lot of one who could offer
them no prizes for their crime save the prospect of misery
or of a bloody death? Against whom then did I raise this
conspiracy? Against the authority whose protection I im-
plore, against the laws the action of which I invoke? And
these great ones of whom you have spoken, my friends, my
patrons . . . are they, too, forming a conspiracy against
the government; they, who have devoted themselves to its
interest? And this royal assembly which with one voice
granted my demand, that, too, belongs to the party conspiring against the government, that assembly formed of the
most distinguished members of all the courts of the realm,
that assembly which has at its head the chief of the whole
magistracy; you know him, gentlemen, he was born in your
midst, brought up in your midst, an honour to you! And
this notary, whose voice was heard with applause by the
Council, and his motion taken up, this man whose name
alone is a panegyric, whose life was ever a reflection of
every religious, political, civil, domestic virtue. This man,
too, is one of the party conspiring against the magistracy—
he, one of its lights and ornaments! And this minister . . .
he likewise is of the party sworn against the magistracy,
he that was born in it, so to speak, who can look round and
see his relations occupying the highest places in it. Yes,
gentlemen, the ministers, the great ones of the kingdom,
the royal council, the philosophers, the historians, whatever

claration of his father's innocence) the memory of the former judges and
accusers would be held up to execration, and that Lally himself was in this
instance acting merely as the spokesman of a set of intriguers. We will draw
attention later to other features of the two famous vindications.

* The Lally family came from Ireland, the name of Tollendal being taken
from the property of Tollendally.

be their class or their country, all are in a conspiracy against the magistracy! And what can I say? There is question, if you believe my opponent, of still greater perils. The King's Majesty is threatened, the throne is tottering, the monarchy imperilled, the kingdom on the verge of destruction, France, Europe, Asia, all gone to ruin, all involved in one general catastrophe, all through neglecting the warnings of this M. d'Epresmenil, and coming ages will bless in him the high-souled saviour who rescued the political world from rushing into chaos!"*

As in the course of the argument, so in rousing the passions the use of contrasts is of service, and they occur frequently in illustrations, and in development, where they are cast into the form of antitheses (see under this figure).†
In moral subjects the introduction often starts *a contrario*.‡

Excellent examples may be found in Cicero *pro Rabirio*, where he shows how little Rabirius's accuser deserves the title of friend of the people: "Quamobrem, uter nostrum tandem, Labiene . . .; read also *in Pisonem*,¶ where he contrasts Piso's and his own consulate; *Cat. 2, 11*, where by comparing the Roman army and Catiline's rabble he stimulates the anger of the Roman people.§

Article II. *Extrinsic Loci* ‖

29. These may all be included under one term *Authority*. Revelation, ecclesiastical and civil legislation, quotations of great men, example;** witnesses, public opinions, history, experience, especially documents, monuments, witnesses, public reports, customs, popular beliefs; all these are at

---

* Speech in answer to Duval d'Epresmenil.
† 103   ‡ c. 4.   ¶ 1, 3-15, 34.
§ Further examples are De Signis, cc. 32, 35, and De Suppl. c. 32, 86; Pro Lege Man. 5, 11.
‖ cf. on this Arist. 1 (νόμοι, νάρτυρες, συνθῆκαι, βάσανοι ὅρκος—all dealing chiefly with forensic eloquence). All these are used by him only as ἄτεχνον in relation to oratorical *discovery* and not to their *treatment*.
** Example (a form of argument proceeding from one or more individual instances to a general law) classed among historical testimonies (authority) when placed among the extrinsic loci, or when treated analogically among the intrinsic loci (argument from analogy), hence παράδειγμα stands also for similitude, etc. See Arist., Rhet. 2, 20; Quintilian, Inst. 5, 11.

the command of the speaker for the development of his proofs.

The authority on which the speaker relies ought to be absolutely *trustworthy, resting on solid foundations* and *accurately interpreted.*

In the use of this source care is to be observed to avoid a dry, monotonous list of quotations as well as a pretentious display of misplaced erudition.

In secular oratory, besides the testimony of reliable authorities, the most frequent use is made of matters relating to *history* and *legislation;* an appeal is made to the law of nature and the prevailing verdict of peoples; also, with caution, to popular sentiment as expressed in all kinds of sayings and instances.

The whole of Æschines's speech against Ctesiphon is an application of the topic a *legibus*, since the argument is based on three laws. In the speech *pro Archia* Cicero draws to a great extent upon the extrinsic loci; so, too, in the speech *pro Milone*, and the same is more or less true of all the forensic speeches.

Examples. Demosthenes, in reply to the assertions made by many that he, indeed, was offering his best advice to the State, but that the latter did not call for words but deeds, says: "I hold that the man who gives advice to you has no business to give any but the best, and that this holds true of the present case, I think I can easily prove. You will recall how Timotheus urged the necessity of helping to save the Eubæans who were being oppressed by the Thebans, and in the course of his address, spoke in more or less the following terms: 'Advise me,' said he, 'come to some decision, as you see the Thebans on the island, what measures you must take. Will you, O Athenians, not cover the seas with your fleet? Will you not rise at once and go down to the Piræus and launch your vessels?' Timotheus spoke, you acted, and as a result the thing was done. He might have given the best possible counsel, as he did, but you might have hesitated and given no heed; could anything then have happened of all the happenings? Impossible. So now in the cause which I am pleading, and which another has pleaded, you must seek for action among yourselves, for the best advice among these who address you.*

There is a splendid passage in the Third Olynthiac contrasting the policy of the Athenians with that of their forefathers: Καίτοι σκέψασθε, ὦ ἄνδρες Ἀθηναῖοι, ἅ τις ἂν κεφάλαι εἰπεῖν ἔχοι τῶν τ'ἐπὶ τῶν προγόνων ἔργων καὶ τῶν ἐφ'ὑμῶν. . . .†

And what force there is in the earlier passage where he holds up to the imitation of the Athenians those who had fallen in the earlier engagements and showed how glorious was their resistance to Philip, though not crowned with success: "No! No! Athenians, you were not misled in facing the danger that threatened the freedom and safety of all. By your ancestors who fought at Marathon, who stood in the lines at Platæa, who maimed the ships at Salamis and at Artemisium, and many others who rest beneath our national monuments, good men and true whom the State buried with equal honours. Not the successful ones only, not the conquerors merely, and justly so. For all alike did a good man's work, though to each fate gave his own lot.‡

Cf. also for this topic, the many eloquent passages in Æschines against Ctesiphon, e.g., on regard for the law: ἐν ὑπολείπεται μέρος τῆς πολιτείας, αἱ τῶν παρανόμων γραφαί;§ on the distinctions accorded to well-deserving citizens in former times (appeal to earlier customs, 177: Ἐπεὶ δε στεφάνων ἀνεμνήσθην); and the one immediately preceding on Solon's law against cowardly soldiers: ὁ γὰρ Σόλον ὁ παλαιὸς νομοθέτης, etc. Further, Demosthenes on the Crown, 248, where he makes a triumphant appeal to the judgement of the Athenians; also Cicero's frequent use of this topic, e.g., the passage quoted earlier on self-defence,‖ the well-known one in *Pro Lege Man.*, "Testis est Italia";¶ and in the same speech** the passage on the slackness of new customs and regulations in the legislation, compared with the similar and popular discourse in Livy (Speech of the tribune Canuleius, 4, 4): "At enim nemo post reges exactos." Flavian makes an

---

* Speech on the situation in the Chersonese (73).   † 23-26.
‡ De Corona, 208.   § In Exord. 5.   ‖ Pro Milone, c. 3, 4.
¶ c.II.   ** 20, sqq.

eloquent appeal to the Emperor Theodosius upon a sentence of Constantine the Great, whose statue had been stoned.*
Also observe the noble reply of Theodosius when granting pardon.

A word on the so-called *Argumentum ad hominem*.

The opponent's handling of a subject or his admissions may supply a proof against him; this is called the *Argumentum ad hominem*.†

Thus Tubero's appearance against Cæsar, Cæsar's behaviour towards his enemies form the subject of the argument in the *Pro Ligario*. See especially his retort to Tubero. He himself has taken up arms against Cæsar: "Who, I ask, says it is a crime to have been in Africa? Evidently he who himself desired to get there and complains because Ligarius prevented him going, and who, notwithstanding, has fought against Cæsar openly. For what was the meaning, O Tubero, of thy drawn sword at the battle of Pharælus? At whose breast was thy dagger pointed? what was the intention of thy weapon? What was thy mind fixed on? Thy hand? Thy lust of battle? What didst thou long for, strive for?"‡

This method is peculiarly applicable in the Refutation. Thus Cicero against Verres, who had put Gavius, a Roman citizen, to death on a cross, and excused himself on the ground that he did not believe the latter's statement that he was a Roman citizen: "Hoc teneo, hic hæreo, judices, hoc sum contentus uno; omitto ac negligo cetera; sua confessione induatar ac juguletur necesse est."§

Cato addressing a portion of the Senate, makes their love of ease an argument against their inactivity in dealing with the Catiline conspiracy, says: "By the immortal gods I appeal to you, who ever value your houses, your estates, your statues, pictures, higher than the State: if you will still keep these things, upon which your whole soul hangs, if you wish to indulge your tastes still further, wake up at once, rally

---

*Extracts, xxii, 3.

† Especially when an argument drawn from the opponent's premises or conclusions can be used against him. We also have: Arg. ad populum, and Arg. ad verecundiam (an appeal to a man's sense of shame or modesty).

‡ 3, 9.

§ De Suppl. 64, 166; the eloquent example in the Extracts, iii, 16.

round the State! It is not a mere question of tribute, nor of some injury to our allies; our freedom, our very lives, are in the balance!"*

A striking example of this argument is to be seen in the speech of Hanno against Mago and Hannibal.†

5. *Hints for the Right Use of the Different Topics*

30. (1) If the subject of the topics, so far as it has been developed here, is to be of any real use to the speaker, he must not apply each topic slavishly, nor in the manner of a school exercise.‡

They ought to act, as we have already observed, merely as signposts, reminders or starting points; the orator should travel over the whole ground with the greatest freedom of mind, without forcing his ideas into a fixed channel by rigidly adhering to them. There can never be question of employing all of them every time; a speech built on such lines would never reveal a mind that had thought out and mastered its subject, nor emotions intensely moved: it would be rather a tiresome hotch potch of ideas strung together, the product of a schoolboy full of commonplaces. Only intelligent meditation stimulated by a judicious employment of the topics can direct the speaker to that richness, and order, and elevation of thought and feeling which mark the real orator. "Cui lecta potenter erit res," says the poet, "nec facundia deseret hunc nec lucidus ordo."§

(2) Which are the topics to call for most attention, the *extrinsic* or the *intrinsic?*

That depends partly on the subject, partly on the point of view taken by the speaker. If the subject is a philosophic *truth*, then the proofs will be philosophic and developed from the *intrinsic loci;* if the subject deals with *facts*, then

---

* Sallust., De Conjur. Cat. 52.   † Livy, 23, 12, 13.

‡ "Whoever seeks his whole salvation in the topics," remarks Schott with some justice (Theorie der Bereds., theil 2, kap. 2, abschn. 2) "runs the risk of becoming pedantic, flat and prolix, and of losing sight of the special object of his discourse, and its relation to the needs of the audience, in the general considerations of the matter."

§ De Arte poet. v, 40.

recourse will be had to the *extrinsic loci*. If the speaker is looking at a question from the *supernatural standpoint* which is always the case in sacred eloquence, the *extrinsic loci*, proofs taken from Holy Scripture, and the authority of the Fathers.

As a general principle it may be laid down that those topics should be chosen which will establish the argument rather than those which serve merely to adorn or fill out the subject. A discourse which is not marked by solidity, which does not give a valid and reasoned line of argument, but drifts into digressions and strings of instances (examples, similes, illustrations) is only a rhetorical display; it may at time strike the imagination, but it can neither convince nor hold the mind.

(3) *Are all these thoughts to be worked up, all these examples to be woven into the discourse, or what choice is to be made?*

Cicero gives the answer; "Multa occurrunt argumenta, multa quæ in dicendo profutura videantur. Sed eorum partim ita levia sunt, ut contemnenda sint; partim etiam si quid habent adjumenti, sunt nonnunquam ejusmodi, ut insit in iis aliquid vitii, neque tanti sit illud, quod prodesse videatur, ut cum aliquo malo conjungantur."

These two categories must hence be completely put aside. "Quæ autem utilia sunt atque firma, si ea tamen (ut sæpe fit) valde multa sunt; ea quæ ex iis aut levissima sunt, aut aliis gravioribus consimilia,* secerni arbitror oportere atque ex oratione removeri. Equidem cum colligo argumenta causarum, non tam ea numerare soleo quam expendere."†

All possible support must be given to the leading thoughts; they must be placed in the clearest light. "Firmissima quæque maxime tueor, sive plura sunt, sive aliquod unum."‡

---

* i.e., such proofs as are quite identical with others and easily lead to repetition.

† De Orat. 2, 76, 308. "As to those arguments which are to the purpose and deserving of trust if they are, as often happens, very numerous, I think that those of them which are of least weight, or as are of the same tendency as others of greater force, ought to be laid aside, and excluded altogether from our pleading. I myself, indeed, in collecting proofs make it a practice *rather* to *weigh* than to *count* them.

‡ De Orat. ii, 72: "I maintain chiefly such as are the strongest, whether there are several or only one.

In actually adopting proofs, the *degree of their cogency* ought to be carefully weighed. According as the proofs are drawn from reason, from personal experience (testimony of the senses), or from the authority of others, they assure *metaphysical, physical* or *moral certitude,* sometimes (when their connexion with indisputable facts is not quite clear) only *probability* in greater or less measure. The speaker must also distinguish between certainties, probable and doubtful proofs; he may exaggerate nothing, nor confuse anything; he must *always weigh his proofs as his opponent would weigh them.* Moreover, just as every thought and every proof have not the same value *per se,* so neither has it in the *judgement of the audience.* Often the importance of a metaphysical proof will escape an uneducated hearer, while on the contrary the force of one drawn from experience, appealing more or less to the senses, will be easily seized upon by him. Cormeninus says with reason: "As a man sees only the largest objects at a distance, *so the majority see only those proofs which leap to the eyes.*"*

§ 6. *Appendix on the Rhetorical Exercises founded on the Topics*

31. In order to reap a practical benefit from the preceding lessons and to avoid drifting into empty and vague recollections of them, it is necessary to do exercises on them or some of them, so as to become familiar with their appearance and use. The trained speaker may use them or not, as he likes, in the working up of his material; for the beginner the method has its distinct advantages and is always conjoined with a system of προγυμνάσματα or exercises. The luminaries of the French pulpit, Bossuet, Bourdaloue, Massillon and other great speakers, all trod the same way. As to the manner of doing these exercises the *most important sources* bearing on a given theme may be examined and employed in framing a *definite and comprehensive range of ideas;* or the *special development* of a theme may be worked out from one or other of the topics. We must here limit ourselves to developing a short example of both methods, which we take from the *Bibliotheca Rhetorum:* †

* Le Livre des Orateurs, i, 11; cf. Cic. de Orat. ii, 38, 139.

† By P. Le Jay, S.J., who taught rhetoric for over thirty years at the

ELOQUENCE

(a) Praise of Justice

1. *General Idea.* Justice is that virtue which inclines us to acknowledge the rights of others. *Philosophical* definition. Justice is the guiding light of states, the terror of evil-doers, the friend of virtue, the foster-mother of peace, the mother of unity, etc. *Rhetorical definition.*

2. *Enumeration of Parts.* Justice preserves the respect of kings, the good name of the nobility, the unity of citizens, the reciprocal trust of the people, the happiness of all; it is a spur to soldiers to obey; a check to evil-doers.

3. *Etymology of the word.* Justice is derived from *just*, because it considers what is just to every one.

4. *Genus.* It is a cardinal virtue, inasmuch as it contains the gifts and graces of other virtues.

5. *Species.* It manifests itself as justice towards God and our neighbours.

6. *Causes.* God is its author (*causa efficiens*), its image again God, the eternal just One (*causa exemplaris*); its object the protection of the just (*causa finalis*).

7. *Effects.* Peace, quietude of the citizens, piety, religious worship, extirpation of vice, planting of virtue, etc.

8. *Comparison.* Justice stands amid virtues like the sun in the firmament; for as the sun disperses the clouds, triumphs over storms and hurricanes, adorns the fields with crops, the trees with fruit, clothes the meadows with smiling green and flowers, and spreads joyfulness over the whole earth, so justice blesses kingdoms with unity, rejoices society with the benefits of peace, etc.

9. *Contrast.* As those peoples, for whom the light of justice has not arisen, lead a wild and rough life, so, on the other hand, those nations who respect justice, excel all others in cultivation and civilization.

10. *Parallel* (*argumentum comparationis a minori ad maius*). If strength, cleverness and the virtues which refer to the well-being of the individual call for universal praise, what

Collège Louis-le-Grand. This work (Paris, 1725, 2 vols) written in flowery Latin, contains among other things a large selection of exercises on the Topics and their application to which we refer here.

commendation does justice, which has for its object the common weal of mankind, deserve?

11. *Proof from the contrary (argumentum a contrario).* Injustice, deceit, oppression, etc., are the ruin of all social order; how very highly should we then value justice, which is opposed to all these disorders.

12. *Extrinsic loci.* The speech may begin with an important utterance of a lawgiver, a philosopher or an orator. A proverb, a parable, a fable, a story or an appropriate example would do equally well.

II. Exhortation to Students to make the most of their Talents

Introduction. Praise of divine Providence, which has made work the chief means of obtaining this world's goods and hence put obstacles in the way of idleness.

Leading Theme. For our consolation it is ordained that we can win everything by work.

Development of the Proofs. (1) Example. A father bequeathed to his son as his only inheritance one field of uncultivated land. Discouraged at the wild state of the plot and at the thought of the heavy labour in store (*imagination*) the son gave himself up to idleness. Then a good friend of the foolish youth interested himself in his behalf and divided the plot into many small plots, every one of which could be easily worked in a day. Whereupon the youth took courage and soon the whole work was finished; the field richly rewarded the care spent upon it. Application to the hearers not to be discouraged by first difficulties.

(2) *Induction.* Industry will turn wild and unfruitful tracts of land into flourishing fields and carve glorious statues out of the marble block, while skilled hands can make the rough diamond the brightest ornament of a royal crown.

(3) *Example.* As an example in point, we have Demosthenes, who overcame natural hindrances to his pronunciation by means of persevering and continuous exercise; Cicero, who by the most strenuous efforts raised himself to the most exalted position; Socrates, who, when sixty years of age, learnt to play the flute.

Conclusion. No one need, therefore, despair of attaining

such a noble object as perfection, provided he is determined to make for it by means of industry and work.

Connected with the above, and on somewhat similar lines, is *Chria*,* which is a scheme for suggesting and developing the main thoughts (*sententia*, γνώμη) on any subject; for example, *Introduction* (or recommendation of the subject to be discussed), *Explanation* or paraphrase, *cause*, *antithesis*, *comparison*, *evidence*, *example*, *epilogue* (application).

* Aphthonius, a rhetorician of Antioch, first formulated this scheme, whence it is called *Chria Aphthoniana;* a shorter and freer form of it (e.g., Introduction, middle, end) is called *Free Chria*, also *Chria Ciceroniana*, of which Cicero gives examples in his Paradoxa, e.g., Paradox 2. M. Seyffert in his Scholæ Latinæ (in which he treats of Chria exhaustively) Part 2, gives instructions and materials for elementary exercises.

CHAPTER II

Means by which the Speaker Pleases and Persuades

32. "If man were guided only by reason," says Father Broeckaert,* "it would suffice to show him the truth, for him to love it; the orator's task would then be confined to discovering and developing the reasons upon which he founded his statement. But his work is to fight, not only against error and ignorance, but against the subtle resistance of the will. The hearer can withdraw himself from the speaker's influence by indulging in indifference and apathy: this is a passive resistance; he may bring to his aid rebellious feelings and a settled attitude of hostility: this is an active resistance. The first form is met by engaging the interest of the hearer, the second by the use of pathos. To win over a man, the speaker must keep ever in view his imagination, his personal interest, and his need for relaxation. The want of attention he must combat by an attractive, lively and picturesque exposition; apathy by an appeal to personal interest; sensitiveness by the gentleness of his oratorical deportment; aversion and disgust by finesse and foresight."

The precepts laid down in the foregoing paragraph call for special attention in settling the style of the discourse and even delivery thereof: in the *choice, too, of the matter* they are of supreme importance, and for that reason we must give them special prominence in this chapter. They affect very profoundly the *manner of developing the subject* and the *value of each element* which goes to form the speech; they furnish the speaker with hints as to the choice of the matter to which he ought to direct his attention. It is most necessary for the orator, at the outset of his career, to be led to a strictly practical way of regarding his work, i.e., to accustom himself to consider his subject, not merely in the general or abstract, but in the concrete and in all its relations, especially those of *psychologic significance*, or in other words to use his

* Guide du jeune Littérateur, III, sect. 2, ch. 1.

knowledge of men. In the following paragraphs we will consider more fully, firstly, how the speaker is to gain a *favourable hearing*, and secondly the *interest* of his audience.

In regard to the first point, it is clear that the speaker should possess the attention of his hearers, if possible even their approval and favour. Want of sympathy or contempt on the part of the audience are rocks on which the best of causes, the ablest of speeches, may suffer shipwreck; on the other hand, good will towards the orator, and trust in his word, finds an echo in the hearts of an audience which helps the speaker's words and lays hold of their hearts and understandings.*

Hence it was ever a maxim of art as well as of nature that the speaker should observe most strictly everything that could exercise any influence in gaining the good will of his hearers, and to avoid most carefully what, in any way, could give just offence; anything that could shock morals, propriety or good taste, or alienate the hearts of the people.

"Caput artis decere," says Cicero;† and Quintilian: "Nec enim alio magis (quam servando quid deceat) animi judicum conciliari, aut si res in contrarium tulit, alienari solent."‡ Aristotle himself, who is so insistent on the development of the proof, is so convinced of the necessity of the point we are treating, as to write, Σχεδὸν ὡς εἰπεῖν, κυριωτάτην ἔχει πίστιν τὸ ἦθος.§

The two chief conditions for gaining and securing the good will of an audience are, the observance of the caution just laid down, known as *oratorical tact*, and as a foundation for it the *honourable, ethical character* of the speech itself.

---

*The most conspicuous example of this is O'Connell. What a magic influence he wielded not only over the hearts of his own countrymen, but over people in Scotland and England, because the spirit of sacrifice for his country which inspired him filled them all with amazement! What assembly ever hung with more awe on the words of a king than the hundreds of thousands who listened to every word from his lips in those monster meetings? Cicero was right— "Nihil est in dicendo majus, quam ut faveat oratori is qui audiet." (De Orat. 2, 42).

†De Orat. 1, 29. In another treatise (Orat. 21) he adds: "Ut in vita, sic in oratore, nihil difficilius est quam *quid deceat* videre."

‡Instit. Or. 11, 1. §1, 2.

MEANS: TO PLEASE AND PERSUADE

§1. *First Means*: *The Moral Character of the Speech*

33. A speaker's moral greatness was always reckoned among the first of his qualifications. Hence the ancient axiom "Nemo orator nisi vir bonus," and Quintilian's definition of the orator: "Vir bonus dicendi peritus"; or in Fénelon's words, "He only deserves to be listened to whose word is enlisted in the service of thought, whose thought is enlisted in the service of truth and virtue."

But it is not sufficient that the orator should have high personal moral qualities; these should be revealed in his words, and this is what Rhetoric includes under the term *mores oratorii*, ἦθος. Its office is to enhance the relation which exists between the character of the speech and the aim contemplated in eloquence. On this ground it goes on to require that the discourse, by virtue of its subject and of the speaker, should always suggest a certain nobility and bear on its brow the stamp of truth and virtue. This character consists, not so much in the words, as in the spirit. Its most prominent features are, as enumerated by Aristotle, *Wisdom, Prudence, Rectitude, Goodwill.**

It presupposes these qualities in the orator, and thus only does it seem natural and unforced. "Prodit enim se, quam? libet custodiatur, simulatio: nec unquam tanta fuerit loquendi facultas, ut non titubet atque hæreat, quotiens ab animo verba dissentiunt. Vir autem malus aliud dicat necesse est quam sentit.... Hoc certe procul eximatur animo, rerum pulcherrimam eloquentiam cum vitiis mentis posse miseri."†

*Τοῦ μὲν οὖν αὑτοὺς εἶναι πιστοὺς τοὺς λέγοντας, τρία ἐστὶ τὰ αἴτια· τοσαῦτα γάρ ἐστι δὶ ἀπιστεύομεν ἔξω τῶν ἀποδείξεων· ἔστι δὲ ταῦτα φρόνησις καὶ ἀρετὴ μαὶ εὔνοια. He proceeds to develop the reason for this enumeration and then adds, Ἀνάγκη ἄρα τὸν ἅπαντα δοκοῦντα ταῦτ' ἔχειν εἶναι τοῖς ἀκροωμένοις πιστόν (Rhet., 2, 1). In fact, the overwhelming impression which true eloquence makes upon us is grounded on this fundamental character of the speech: moral elevation is also the purest source of true pathos.

† "Simulation, however guarded, always betrays itself, nor was there ever so much power of eloquence in any man that he would not falter and hesitate whenever his words were at variance with his thoughts. But a bad man must of a necessity utter words at variance with his thoughts. ... At least let this notion be wholly banished from our minds, that perfect eloquence, the noblest of human attainments, can be united with a vicious character." Quint. 12, 1, 29–32. So far Quintilian is right, as *finished* eloquence can only be found in a noble man; "Non igitur unquam malus homo et perfectus orator." Can the

ELOQUENCE

§ 2. *Second Means. Oratorical Tact*

34. Under this heading is included the studious regard of those many circumstances in which the orator finds himself where his prudence, his fine feeling, his position, his demeanour, his knowledge of men demand of him that he should keep his energies ever fixed upon the one subject of gaining the ear of his auditors and drawing them to his view. We may distinguish three elements, *oratorical propriety*, oratorical *precaution* and the awakening of *interest*. Careful attention must be paid to all these matters, both in the choice of subject and the moral character of the speech; in fact, they may be said to be nothing more than the outcome of the latter.

I. *Oratorical Propriety* (Τὸ Πρέπον, *Decorum*)

35. By this term is understood the perfect adaptation of thought and feeling, of speech and delivery, even of the very silence of the speaker, to his subject, to the development thereof, and to his audience, in effect, to all the circumstances which may attend his discourse. Here again the maxim is supreme: *Caput artis decere.* The observance of oratorical decorum is no slight strain upon the culture, the taste, the tact and experience of the orator.*

Hence he must keep before his eyes:

(1) *His own personality:* his position, his years, his dignity, his reputation. "Ipsum etiam eloquentiæ genus alios aliud decet. . . . Est quod principes deceat, aliis non concesseris. Idem dictum sæpe in alio liberum, in alio furiosum, in alio superbum est." †

Christian orator lag behind the heathen in his morals! A striking example of how low the depths to which talent may sink, when deprived of the inspiration of truth and virtue, is to be seen in the case of Mirabeau, who, when he speaks in defence of law and order, presents features of real eloquence (as in the addresses, " Sur le veto, sur le droit de paix et de guerre, sur la contribution du quart,") but when he acts as the hireling of falsehood, offers the spectacle of a mere demagogue flinging abroad empty, bombastic phrases without logic or culture.

* The enthusiasm, inseparable from eloquence, caused the ancients to recognize its symbol in the honey-bearing bee. Homer says of "sweetly spoken " Nestor that " from his lips flowed speech sweeter than honey." Νέστωρ ἡδυεπὴς . . . τοῦ καὶ ἀπὸ γλώσσης μέλιτος γλυκίων ῥέεν αὐδή.—Il. a, 249; and Theocritus gives his Thyrsus a mouthful of honey (Idyll. 2, 146). See Wenkelmann's Werke, 9. Versuch einer Allegorie, bes. für d. Kunst, 103.

†Quint., Inst. Or. 11, 1, 31–37.

One of the most usual pitfalls of the speaker is *Vanity;* the wish to be brilliant and to please, hence *affectation* in style, voice, attitude, action. "Imprimis omnis vitiosa jactatio est, eloquentiæ tamen in oratore præcipue; affertque audientibus non fastidium modo, sed plerumque etiam odium."

With a little discrimination and by avoiding what is unbecoming, even a person of moderate talents has the power of engaging and touching the heart. "Quibus a natura minora data sunt," observes Cicero, "tamen illud assequi possunt, ut iis quæ habent, modice et scienter utantur."*

Great orators have always acknowledged modesty to be a necessary quality even when compelled to speak to their own advantage. "Intelligo," says Cicero, "quam scopuloso difficilique in loco verser. Nam cum omnis arrogantia odiosa est, tum illa ingenii atque eloquentiæ multa molestissima."†

Demosthenes in his speech on the Crown apologizes for the freedom with which he is obliged to talk of himself, by the necessity forced upon him of answering the charges brought against him by Æschines, and proceeds: "I will endeavour to treat this question with the greatest restraint, but, whatever the occasion forces upon me, *he* (*Æschines*) is responsible for having pressed the contest upon me."

When Cicero had to prove that he was more fitted than Cæcilius to undertake the persecution of Verres, instead of praising himself, he enlarged upon the qualities which were required in an undertaking of this scale, and added that he had devoted his whole life to pursuits and business of this kind; if then he could not flatter himself on possessing the requisite skill, much less could Cæcilius claim it. "Perhaps you may say, what then! Are you endowed with all these qualifications? I wish indeed that I were; but at all events I have laboured from my very childhood to attain them. And if on account of the magnitude and difficulty of such a study I have not been successful, although I have striven for them all my life: how far distant from them must you be." ‡

Unfortunately, Cicero did not always preserve this modesty, and but too frequently betrayed his self-appreciation.

(2) *The Audience.* Its rank, culture, age, morals, foibles,

---

* De. Orat. 1, 29.   † In Cæcil. 11, 36.   ‡ In Cæcil. 12. 40.

habits, beliefs, nationality, temper—these are to be fully gauged by the speaker. "Nec tantum *quis* et *pro quo*, sed etiam *apud quem* dicas interest. . . . Nec eadem apud principem, magistratum, senatorem, privatum, tantum liberum, ratio est . . . non idem apud eruditum, quod militarem ac rusticum deceat."*

These remarks of Quintilian concern not only the avoiding of all that is unbecoming, but, like the notes on time and place which follow, indicate the prudent use of all that conduces to the speaker's object in the attitude, temper, etc., of the audience.

Livy relates of Hannibal that before the battle of Zama he addressed the different sections of his army in words best suited to the nationality and temper of each one of them:† to the allies, besides their usual pay, he promised a large share of the spoil; in the Gauls he roused up their long-standing hatred against the Roman name; to the Legarians he pictured the smiling plains of Italy in contrast with the desolate mountains on which they dwelt; with the Mauri and Numidians he dwelt on the tyrannical rule of Masinissa; and on the Carthaginians he pressed the urgency of fighting for the defence of their country, their household gods, the graves of their fathers, for the lives of their parents, their wives and their children.

More especially must the orator be on his guard in his attitude towards those whom he has to blame or refute; not only must he avoid any want of justice and charity but he must suggest, by his expression and bearing, complete remoteness from all that is vulgar or has the appearance of unrestrained passion. Let him always keep in mind Quintilian's beautiful expression: "Jucundissima in homine humanitas, facilitas, moderatio, benevolentia."‡

---

* "Nor is it of importance only what our own character is, and for whom we plead, but to whom we address ourselves. . . . The gravity of the senate demands one sort of eloquence, and the levity of the popular assembly another. . . . The same manner that is proper in speaking to a man of learning is improper when addressing a soldier or an uneducated man."—Quint., 11, 1, 13-15.   † 30, 33.

‡ "The qualities that will recommend him most are courtesy, mildness, good temper and benevolence."—11, 1, 42.

In this respect the greatest orators of ancient times, Demosthenes and Æschines in their contests, Cicero against Piso, etc., have been guilty of glaring breaches of propriety: of course they may not have broken any of the conventions, as these were understood at a time when a speaker was allowed remarkable freedom in this respect; but they did not comply with the absolute dictates of humanity.

(3) *Time and Place.* Special character, meaning for the audience, remembrances awakened, etc. "Nam et tempus tum triste, tum lætum, tum liberum, tum angustum est, atque ad hæc omnia componendus orator: et loco publico privatone, celebri an secreto, aliena civitate an tua, in castris denique an foro dicas, interest plurimum, ac suam quidque formam et proprium quendam modum eloquentiæ poscit."*

(4) *The personality of those about whom the orator is speaking,* whether the address deals with other people or their affairs, whether praising or blaming or introducing only the mere mention of them, the speaker should always observe a due regard for propriety, truth, moderation, both in the subject and his manner of treating it.

II. *Oratorical Precaution (Cautio).*

36. It is not enough that the speaker should never violate the rules of propriety; certain matters in themselves irreproachable, are not appropriate, or demand a special preparation with a view to being received well by the audience, or to avoid causing undesirable protests or awakening bitter feeling.

Thus oratorical precaution is peculiarly necessary:

(1) When the hearer or something connected with him is to be criticized. He must be convinced of the good will and charity which is entertained for him; what can be excused must be excused; the criticism itself is to be dexterously intro-

---

* Quint. 11, 1, 46-47. Cf. Cic., Orat. 21,22. By way of making the speaker familiar with the demands of place, time and people, Aristotle treats with great practical acumen the question of morals, and particularly in their fourfold relation to the passions (Rhet. 2, 2-11, ἕξεις) and the varying conditions of age and fortune (ἡλικίαι, τύχαι, 2, 12-17); and for the use of the political orator, he deals also with the different forms of government (1, 8).

Cf. the Exordia of Cicero's speeches pro Marcello, pro Lege Manilia, pro Milone.

duced, not pushed too far, and the real good which is in the hearer must not be lost sight of.

"Ut semel plura complectar"—this precept of Quintilian, so like one of the beautiful Gospel sayings, may be taken as a summing up all the rules that embrace this portion of the subject—"nunquam decebit sic adversus tales agere personas, quomodo contra nos agi ab hominibus conditionis ejusdem iniquo tulissemus."*

Scipio, in his address to his rebellious soldiers, speaks forcibly and sternly yet with the greatest tact: "Indeed, if I thought that the whole army were unanimous in desiring my death, this very moment I would die in your presence; for of what value would be a life hateful to my soldiers and fellow-citizens? Probably the main body is moved only as the sea is by the wind, and that the storm is only on the surface without invading the calm depths. The beginning of this foolish revolt must be sought for in its originators; you have allowed yourselves to be contaminated."

Quintilian deduces the following rules from observations of Cicero's dealings with Cato and Servius Sulpitius, whose views he had to combat, while defending Murena's cause: "Cum aliquid detrahere, salva gratia, velis, concedas alia omnia; in hoc solo vel minus peritum quam in ceteris, adjecta, si poterit fieri, etiam causa, cur id ita sit, vel paulo pertinaciorem, vel credulum, vel iratum, vel impulsum ab aliis. Hoc illis commune remedium est, nisi in tota actione æqualiter appareat non honor modo, sed etiam caritas; præterea causa sit nobis justa sic dicendi; neque id moderate tantum faciamus, sed etiam necessario."† Cicero himself

---

* "And to say much in a few words—it would never be seemly to plead against such persons in a style which we should not like others to use against us."—11, 1, 66-68.

† "When you wish to deny a person any particular excellence without offending him, grant him every other good quality, observing that in this respect alone he is less judicious than in the others, adding, if possible, the reason for this—as that he has been a little too obstinate, or credulous, or angry, or that he is incited by other persons. This may serve as a common remedy for qualifying our language in all such cases, if there appear, through the whole of our argument, a regard for not only what is honourable but for what is kind."—11, 1, 71-72.

says with regard to the last injunction: "Si quid persequare acrius, ut invitus et coactus, facere videare."[*]

Quintilian also adds a further warning on the imprudence of attacking *whole communities;* when the speaker is forced to use terms of blame against such bodies or whole nations, the following advice is offered as worthy of consideration: "Commune remedium est ut ea quæ lædunt non libenter tractare videaris, nec in *omnia* impetum facias, sed in *id quod expugnandum est;* et reprehendens *alia laude compenses.*"[†]

As in the case of communities or nations, so too in social and moral relations, where dignities, rights, principles, etc., are involved, the speaker must be heedful that he does not give the impression of invading them or betraying a want of impartiality. This may happen, e.g., when discussing the duties of inferiors towards those placed over them, or vice versa, of parents to children, of authorities to subjects, etc.

Cicero supplies a beautiful example in his speech *pro Cluentio*, where he has to defend the latter for having appeared as the accuser of his own mother: "You have heard the origin of these strained relations with his mother ... I know very well that no matter what the character of a mother may be, it does not become a son to speak before the court of her wickedness. I should not, O judges, be fit to conduct any case, if, when I was employed in defending a friend from danger, I were to fail to see what is deeply implanted in the heart of all men by nature. I am quite aware that it is right for men not only to be silent as to what injuries they suffer from their parents, but even to bear them with equanimity. Yet I think what is bearable ought to be borne, and what can be buried in silence ought to be kept so."[‡]

(2) When the audience is possessed by prejudice or ill-feeling against the *speaker* or the *subject*, the ill-feeling should be borne with, and not attacked too brusquely; rather an attempt should be made to approach the point of view of the audience; or where this cannot be done, the principle assumed, that every one *is willing to surrender* and

[*]De Orat. 2, 43, 82.   [†]11, 87-91.   [‡] Pro Cluent. 6.

thus *gradually mitigate* the prejudices which militate against the speaker's cause.

When Antony undertook to rouse the people against Brutus and Cassius and the rest of the conspirators who had murdered Cæsar, he made no direct and open attack upon their indignation against the latter, nor their love for Brutus and Cassius, but appeared in their presence with sorrowful mien, and begged them to excuse his tears; he had no intention of blaming the conspirators for the death of Cæsar; no doubt that was merely the result of their endeavour to be of service to the State; but did Cæsar deserve so tragic a fate? He who was always so generous, so highminded in dealing with his enemies! After making this breach in their dislike, he takes the offensive. Cæsar's murderer, he exclaims, was Brutus, Cæsar's son! for every Roman was counted by Cæsar as his son and heir of his possessions. . . . Then using the people's new attitude of good will and sympathy with Cæsar to urge them to vengeance, he uncovers the blood-stained corpse and calls the people to arms. The passage which we can only give, unfortunately, in outline, shows a great knowledge of the human heart.

Compare Shakespeare's development of the idea.

(3) When the subject has *tragic features* or such as affect the audience with emotions of *grief* or *shame*, it should be treated *indirectly* rather than *directly*, by means of an *illustration*, an *historical parallel*, a *pregnant phrase*, etc. At times even the thing itself will not bear mention. "Eadem res sæpe aut probatur aut reicitur, alio atque alio elato verbo."*

Cicero very cleverly disentangled himself from a difficult position when replying to Tubero's accusation. He could not, nor did he wish to deny the fact that Ligarius and he, Cicero himself, had avowed themselves the enemies of Cæsar; yet on the other hand, for fear of affronting the Pompeian party, he could not acquiesce in the term *scelus*, with which Tubero had stigmatized their former attitude towards Cæsar, and which now formed the chief point of Tubero's accusation.

"You call that a crime, Tubero? Why so? This cause has never yet been stigmatized by that name. Some call it a mis-

---

* Cic., Orat. 22.

take; some fear; others who give it a harder name term it hope, ambition, hatred, obstinacy, and those who are more severe still, rashness; but up to the present no one except you has ever called it a crime. My own opinion is, if anyone seeks for a proper and accurate name for our misfortune, that some fateful influence descended upon and seized the shortsighted minds of men; so that no one ought to wonder that human counsels were overruled by divine necessity."*

These words contain nothing that could wound the Pompeians, while they are most complimentary to Cæsar.

Examples on what has been said above

37. Since oratorical tact is of such immense importance and is better illustrated by examples than by precept, we will make a special study of two examples which are peculiarly fitted to illustrate the rules already laid down.

The first is the speech which Livy puts into the mouth of Capitolinus, when it came to the last extremity of urging the people to sink their differences with the Senate and unite their forces against the Aequians and Volscians, who were besieging the city;† the second specimen is the introduction to Cicero's second speech against the Agrarian Law.

(1) To gain his object Capitolinus had to overcome three obstacles; in the first place, he had to conquer the ill-feeling entertained against the patrician order, of which he himself was a member; he had, moreover, to draw the people away from the tribunes, who were all-powerful; and finally he had to show the people how unjust was their attitude towards the Senate.

How did he gain his point? It is not enough for him to go forth and meet a raging mob with mildness; it is more than humiliating for him, that, in his fourth Consulate, his country's enemies should be pressing up to the very walls of Rome.

He first endeavours to disarm the people of the excuse they found for their inactivity in the pride of the patricians by humbling himself, the head of the order, in their eyes; at the same time he rouses their sentiment of patriotism, the most powerful motive he could appeal to in their present temper; he says nothing of the disunion in the State

*Pro. Ligar. 6. 17.   †3, 67.

but confines himself to the bold advance of the enemy. "Etsi mihi nullius noxæ conscius, Quirites, sum tamen cum pudore summo in concionem vestram processi. Hoc vos scire, hoc posteris memoriæ traditum iri, Æquos et Volscos vix Hernicis modo pares, T. Quinctio quartum consule ad mænia urbis impune armatos venisse!" etc.

While continuing to fan the flame he had lighted, he goes on to the causes of the present humiliating situation, but without referring to the chief of them—the present split. "Quem tandem ignavissimi hostium contempsere? Nos consules? An vos Quirites? si culpa in nobis est, auferte imperium indignis; et si id parum est, insuper pænas expetite. Si in vobis"—here, with great feeling, he rejects the idea of punishment falling on the people and gives expression to the good will that lingers within him—"nemo deorum nec hominum sit qui vestra puniat peccata, Quirites: vosmet tantum eorum pœniteat." Although, in contrasting them with the Senate, he has already flattered the people as much as their vanity could desire, he does not yet venture upon the reproaches which he has to make to them; instead of that he reminds them of their seasoned courage, of their victories over those who are now besieging them: "Non illi vestram ignaviam contempsere, nec suæ virtuti confisi sunt; quippe toties fusi fugatique, castris exuti, agro mulctati, sub jugum missi, et se at vos novere."

At last he comes to the cause of all the trouble—"discordia ordinum." Still, he does not assert that all the blame lies with the people; half of it lies at the door of the Senate and he accuses himself and it: "Dum nec nobis imperii nec vobis libertatis est modus. . . ." This is now magnificently carried through. The speaker starts off with energy and decision; he shows how often the people by their unruly conduct have betrayed themselves, their interests, their honour; how much nobler was their behaviour on other occasions; how the city and the State are on the way to ruin if they persist in their turbulence and dissension. Then for fear of leaving an unfavourable impression on their minds by the vehemence of his words, he explains that he has spoken so strongly out of his love for them and the country: "His ego gratiora dictu alia esse scio, sed me vera pro gratis loqui, etsi ingenium non moneret, necessitas cogit. Vellem equidem vobis placere, Quirites, sed multo malo vos salvos esse, qualicunque erga me animo futuri estis. . . ."

To this noble expression of feeling, in which the speaker follows Demosthenes, succeeds the last decisive passage aimed at the favourites of the people, the tribunes, with the promise of victory, if they will but follow his advice.

(2) Cicero, when raising his voice to oppose the Agrarian Law, had before him as difficult a task as that of Capitolinus. The distribution of the land was a bait by which the tribunes drew the people into sympathy with their revolutionary plans; to the people the measure was an access of freedom, a pledge of future well-being. Cicero had been appointed Consul by the acclamation of the people, and had in consequence to think how he might prove to them his appreciation of the favour; while to proceed against the Agrarian Law meant the inflaming of every passion against him. How then did he tackle the situation? He opens his speech with a glowing recognition of the extraordinary kindness which he has received at the hands of the Roman people, and couples with it, the assertion that it will always be his first care to be a really popular Consul, a friend of the people in the very best meaning of the term. He finds, however, that the expression *popularis* needs some explanation on account of the frequent misuse to which the term is exposed: " Sed mihi ad hujus verbi vim et interpretationem vehementer opus est vestra sapientia." He then goes on to show what the true meaning is, and on the other hand, the meaning which it has acquired in the minds of some (the tribunes) who, under the fair disguise of the people's welfare, conceal their own wicked plans directed against that welfare. He comes to the Agrarian Law. He is careful to avoid attacking it as such, and concedes that there can be good Agrarian Laws: "Nam at vere dicam, Quirites, genus ipsum legis agrariæ vituperare non possum. Venit enim mihi in mentem duos clarissimos, ingeniosissimos, amantissimos plebis Romanæ viros, Tib. et C. Gracchos, plebem in agris publicis constituisse."

By praising these two famous leaders of the people Cicero very dexterously avoids the accusation of being opposed to the tribunes on all points. He explains now how the present law must be regarded askance because its patrons, in spite of their frank declarations that they wished to unite their efforts with his for the welfare of the people, had always carefully excluded him from all nearer acquaintance; in their assemblies as in public measures they had always guarded their real plans from the light of day and from outside criticisms, etc.; that when the law was placed before the people and had come into his hands he had tried honestly and courageously to defend it, striving to see good in it; but he had discovered that nothing was given to the people, on the contrary, that their former liberty was withdrawn from them, and a decemvirate introduced under a popular name, etc. Yet he was not anxious to press upon the people this, his view of the law, rather, in case they did not see eye to eye with him he would surrender his contention and join them: " Quæ quum exposuero, si falsa vobis videbuntur esse; sequar auctoritatem vestram, mutabo meam sententiam. Sin insidias fieri libertati vestræ, simulatione largitionis, intelligetis: nolitote dubitare plurimo sudore et sanguine majorum vestrorum partam vobisque traditam libertatem, nullo vestro labore, consule adiutore, defendere."*

Cicero triumphed. Pliny the Elder says of this splendid triumph of eloquence:"Te dicente legem agrariam, hoc est alimenta sua, abdicaverunt tribus."†

III. *The Arousing of Interest*

38. By this term we mean the living share which the audience takes in the speech, and we call it Oratorical because of its connexion with the speech.

(1) The *first* and *most usual way* of arousing attention and interest in a subject is to enlarge upon its *magnitude* and *importance.*

Cicero does this skilfully in the introduction to his fourth speech against Verres, where he has to comment on the latter's robberies: "I come now to what Verres himself calls his *zeal;* what his friends call his disease, his madness; what

* Leg. Agrar. 2, 1-6.   † Hist. Nat. 7, 30.

the Sicilians call his rapine; how I am to describe it, I know not. I will state the whole affair to you, and do you judge it on its own merits and not on the name applied to it. First of all, gentlemen, let me give you an account of this conduct of his, then, perhaps, you will not have far to seek in giving it a name."

(2) The *second means* of awakening interest is to *demonstrate* the *similarity* which exists between the subject or person spoken of to the circumstances or condition of the audience. Most true is Broeckaert's observation: "Our attention is always keenly alive to everything that brings before us in any way an actual or possible phase of human destiny, and so to speak reflects our own position. To this is due in part the interest that we take in the drama, in poetry, in panegyrics, in likenesses, in examples, in accounts of customs, etc."

This motive, too, Cicero knew how to turn to account, especially in his speech *de Suppliciis* where he describes, not only the plundering of the Navarchs and Gavius, but makes the cause of the former identical with that of the allies of Rome and Gavius. "Per deos immortales! judices, quo tandem animo sedetis, aut hæc quemadmodum auditis? Utrum ego desipio et plus, quam satis est, doleo tanta calamitate miseriaque sociorum? an vos quoque hic acerbissimus innocentium cruciatus et mæror pati sensu doloris afficit?"* And in regard to Gavius: "Non tu (Verres) hoc loco Gavium, non unum hominem, nescio quem civem Romanum, sed communem libertatis et civitatis causam in illum cruciatum et crucem egisti. . . ."† See also the remarkable passage in *pro Flacco*, "de salute omnium nostrum de fortunis civitatis," etc.‡ . . . With great art Demosthenes in his speech on the Crown keeps his own cause constantly identified with that of the Athenians, and brings into prominence the intimate connexion which always subsisted between his own thoughts and deeds and their views and decisions. We have another beautiful example of this deep psychological development in Veturia's speech to Coriolanus.§

Count Lally-Tollendal opens his speech in defence of the

* 46, 123 sq.   † 66, 170.   ‡ 94, 100.   §Liv. 2, 40.

memory of his father, who had been wrongfully condemned, in the following words: "The cause of the unhappy is the cause of all mankind; the cause of the innocent is the cause of all ages; to-day I bring both before the judgement of the world. A citizen of the wide world, forced to call my fatherland the place where I find an asylum, and until now detained in this country by the kindness of its rulers, and the hope of fulfilling the holiest of my duties, I lay the history of my sufferings before the assembly of humanity, before Europe which permitted them, before France which caused them, before the King who can repair them, before posterity which will judge of them. Soldiers, statesmen, citizens, men whoever you be, if you love justice you will join your voices with mine in the cause of slandered truth, of persecuted virtue, of injured humanity. You especially, dutiful and obedient sons, who perform with joyous zeal the duties of that privileged condition, you, tender and loving fathers, who in security, enjoy the raptures of that sweet name, you will plead with me for a father who was doomed to destruction without the chance of defending himself, for a son who was made unfortunate before he could learn the extent of his loss!"

(3) The *third* and most powerful means is *personal interest*, which keeps before the audience the immediate or remote connexion between the subject and their own well-being, security, etc.

Demosthenes is master of the method, and this motive of personal interest is the keynote of all the Philippics; unceasingly he rouses the Athenians from their sluggishness by picturing to them the greatness of the dangers which press upon them by their own fault. By following up his pictures of, e.g., their sloth, their cross purposes with the facts of their losses, he gives double effect to his words. Compare, for instance, the following passage from the First Philippic: Ἦ βούλεσθε, εἰπέ μοι, περμόντες . . . "Ὥσπερ δὲ οἱ βάρβαροι πυκτεύουσι . . . Ἃμ᾽ ἀκηκόαμέν τι.*

A good specimen is to be seen in Mirabeau's speech on the Fourth of the Income, Brougham's on the Reform Bill,

* 10, 40, 36.

the conclusion of Montalembert's appeal for freedom of education, and in the whole series of O'Connell's discourses to the inhabitants of the United Kingdom, in which with compelling energy and profound knowledge of human nature, appeal is made, at one time to personal interests, at another to the universal human interests involved in those personal interests. Lally-Tollendal finishes up the speech which we quoted above by the following words addressed to Louis XVI: "Oh, no! the voice of misfortune wedded to innocence will never be raised in vain. Your Majesty knows that the blood of the just man cries to heaven when it is not heard on earth. You will see that not to avenge it is to shed that blood again. You will tear out of the history of France that page of injustice which the rest of the world holds up to our reproach; a judgement in which every one saw the punishment, but none recognized the crime; a judgement, in fine, which exists as a monument of injustice and ingratitude to a commander, who, least of all, expected that reward for his services; a monument of fear and of terror to all who follow in his steps. One and the same utterance will avenge the injury done to an innocent man, and appease the trouble of his soul. The defenders of our country, freed from the anxiety lest their efforts should be made a crime, will gladly give themselves to that whole-hearted devotion which our soldiers have ever displayed to their monarch; and if the blessings poured out from a grateful heart can call down upon kings the love of the Most High, upon those who do more by their good deeds than by their power; then what treasures of glory and happiness will be bestowed on a monarch for whom appeal is made to the Almighty by a son who is delivered from the greatest of woes; by whole classes of his subjects, who are freed from all menace; by virtue herself declared spotless; by all mankind, ever ready to uphold its rights and sustain the law, and to banish all that leads to the destruction of the one and the abuse of the other!"

(4) *Fourth means,* effectual on æsthetic grounds, is the use of *illustration* or *picture-forming.*

Illustration is an excellent mode of giving force to

the above methods, and all great speakers have been distinguished for its use. Fénelon says of it: "The whole of eloquence can be reduced to three points: *proving, illustrating, moving.*" * "By illustration," says Cormenin,† "eloquence has produced its greatest results. The panegyric of Demosthenes over those who fell at Marathon, the shameful treatment of Roman citizens at the hands of Verres, as described by Cicero; the night of terror in which Henrietta's death came like a thunder-clap, as pictured by Bossuet; the avenging dust of Marius; the 'De l'audace! De l'audace! toujours de l'audace!' of Danton; the Republic, 'which like Saturn devours her children,' of Vergniaud; the cry of the lakes and mountains of O'Connell—there is the eloquence of pictures."

Cicero painted in glowing colours Pompey's greatness as a general; forced at the same time to speak of Lucullus, whose military talents it is no part of his plan to panegyrize, he pictures fairly but in subdued tones his feats of arms and presents him as a competent commander, while Pompey is held up to the wonder and admiration of the people as an incomparable leader.‡

This sort of picture-making demands a *great subject* and an *imposing setting.* Unlike the class of illustration such as would befit ordinary prose composition, the kind of which we speak here ought first and foremost to be in harmony with the object for which the speaker is pleading; he will paint war in one way, when he wishes to bring out the features of energy, of confusion, of horror . . . ; in another, when he paints it as a judgement of God or as the medium of blessings directed by a higher Providence; in another way again, when he uses it to demonstrate the peculiar qualities of a nation; and in still another manner when he makes it the means of demonstrating the heroic qualities of a commander.

From among the many features which are adapted to the

---

* Quite right in the sense that the art of illustration is a powerful element in oratory; only partially true, however, in the sense (according to Fénelon) that *placere* should supply for the whole of the speech.

† *Livre des Orateurs,* 2.   ‡ Pro Lege Man. 8, 11.

goal aimed at by the speaker, he will choose only a few of the most pertinent, and will bind these into a beautiful whole with an energetic brevity, a lively swing, and compelling movement. The picture should not be a lifeless tableau, a rigid mosaic; it demands the historic stamp, animation, and leads on the hearer or the reader by the hand as it were, through the windings of a dell, or by the edge of a stream, through the serried files of an army, or the wild confusion of a country at war.

Of Cicero's many pictures, several of which occur in the present work, we draw attention only to the following: *pro Milone*, 32 (Clodius's profligacy); *pro Doma sua*, 23 (the slights inflicted on Cicero's household); *Phil.* 2, 25 (Antony's enormities); *de Suppliciis* (the descent of the pirates on Syracuse, Verres's cruelty to the ship captains and their relations, Gavius's crucifixion; where especially narrative and illustration are woven together, and the one helps, carries on and enlivens the other). A brief oratorical picture is supplied in the following extract from Lally's Defence of Louis XVI: "Whatever be the feelings that divide man from man, ought not at least humanity to bind them together? Oh, who can escape it when he contemplates this awful descent from the height of human greatness into the abyss of ghastly sorrow! When he sees how these noble victims of disaster have been given over for the last three years to all the horrors of political fury, have been dashed from rock to rock, from shipwreck to shipwreck, now touching shore, now hustled back time after time into the waves, forlorn waifs drifting on a furious sea, clasping the last plank that remains to them."

Let us quote also from Burke's Speech on the Nabob of Arcot's Debts:

"While the authors of all these evils were idly and stupidly gazing on this menacing meteor, which blackened all their horizon, it suddenly burst and poured down the whole of its contents upon the plains of the Carnatic. Then ensued a scene of war, the like of which no eye hath seen, no heart conceived, and which no tongue can adequately tell. All the horrors of war before known or heard of were mercy to the new havoc. A storm of universal fire blasted every field, consumed every house, destroyed every temple. The miserable inhabitants, flying from their flaming villages, in part were slaughtered; others without regard to sex, to age, to the respect of rank, or sacredness of function; fathers torn from children, husbands from wives, enveloped in a whirlwind of cavalry, and amid the goading spears of drivers and the trampling of pursuing horses were swept into captivity in an unknown and hostile land."

CHAPTER III

Rhetorical Means by which the Speaker moves his Audience.
Passions. Emotions

39. The essential for the establishing of a proposition or a
truth, is the *proof;* hence Aristotle's expression already
quoted: Αἱ γὰρ πίστεις ἔντεχνόν ἐστι μόνον· τὰ δ'ἄλλα
προσθῆκαι.

The concern of the speaker is not the *theoretical* but the
practical driving home of the truth. It is not enough for him
to gain the assent of the intellect, his goal is the will; in
short, he stands out not as a philosopher but as a pleader;
hence, every means by which he can lead man's passions
and increase his skill in elevating and influencing them, is
of the greatest importance; *they decide the victory.* "Probare,"
says Cicero, "necessitatis est; delectare suavitatis; flectere,
victoriæ.* Of the power of exciting the feelings he adds immediately afterwards:"In quo sunt omnia, in quo vis omnis
oratoris est."†

§1. *Of the Passions in general*
First Article. *Their Importance*

40. *Passion* (oratorical pathos) is the term by which every
strong sensation of the soul is described.

Usually the orator is stirred to passion by his intimate
knowledge of the motives, and it is only his strength of
feeling combined with these motives that will impress the
audience. Success in carrying conviction is often dependent
on the strength of the passions aroused. Orators of mediocre
ability frequently err, because they think that the mere
enumeration of the motives is sufficient to arouse the passions. And yet how truly Cicero says: "Nec unquam is, qui
audiret, incenderetur nisi ardens ad eum perveniret oratio!"‡
Even solid motives unless animated by the entire strength
and devotion of the feelings are not enough, at least not for
the masses.‖

---

* Orat. 21, 69.   † Orat. 21; de Orat. 2, 53, 215.   ‡ Orat. c. 38, 132.

‖ Nothing is so contrary to sense as a studied pathos. It may, therefore,
appear rather strange to treat of the theory of the rousing of the emotions,

ELOQUENCE

For this reason all great orators and teachers of Eloquence have given the *pathetic* such a prominent position. An old rhetorician says: "I can with all confidence assert that nothing renders a speech more sublime, than noble, purposeful and enthusiastic emotion; this breathes into it the heat of a higher inspiration and fills it with a certain, almost superhuman strength." And Cicero says: "Quis non fateatur, quum ex omnibus oratoris laudibus longe ista sit maxima, inflammare animos audientium et quocunque res postulet modo, flectere, qui hac virtute caruerit, id ei, quod maximum fuerit, defuisse."*

Only eloquence, such as streams forth from the overflowing source of absolute belief in his subject, deserves the following glorious praise of the Roman orator: "Tantam vim habet illa, quæ recte a bono poeta dicta est flexanima atque omnium regina rerum oratio, ut non modo inclinantem excipere aut stantem inclinare, sed etiam adversantem et repugnantem, ut imperator bonus ac fortis, capere possit."†

Hence in the beautiful words of Quintilian: "Huc igitur incumbat orator, hoc opus ejus, hic labor est, sine quo cætera nuda, jejuna, infirma, ingrata sunt: adeo velut spiritus operis hujus atque animus est in affectibus."‖

and to subject them to cold criticism. But there is no other means of giving to the intending orator a correct understanding of the hidden working of nature, and of gaining for him sure footholds in this the most difficult part of eloquence, the technical treatment of the pathetic element. In the interests of thorough knowledge, criticism analyses musical harmony, it analyses the most affecting passages of poetry; in fact, every art has its peculiar science of correct taste. And never are taste and judgment so necessary as in cases where, instead of the quiet flow of reason, the passions in a certain measure, hold sway. A pedantic study of the passions, instead of being a guide, may sometimes lead to affectation and render it difficult to rise to the occasion, but a *psychological* study will never have this effect. If anyone thinks that Horace's "Si vis me flere" contains the sum of knowledge of the correct rules of pathos, he has certainly never had a teacher's experience of the difficulties which a beginner finds in the management of this division of eloquence.

* Brutus, 80, 279.   † De Orat. 2, 44, 187.

‖ 6, 2, 7. Every speech must be founded on emotion, but whether, in a particular case, it is of more importance to stir up the emotions or to convince

Second Article. *Passions—Genera*

41. (1) The *origin* of the emotions is twofold: the *desire for some good thing* or *the aversion to some evil thing*. Philosophers trace these passions back to love and hatred, or merely to love, as the source of all inner emotions. The ancients distinguish particularly: *voluptas, molestia, metus, cupiditas*. Cicero* says: "Hæc fere maxime sunt in judicum animis, aut quicunque illi erunt, apud 'quos agemus, oratione molienda, amor, odium, iucundia, invidia, misericordia, spes, lætitia, timor, molestia."

(2) *According to their strength* the passions are divided into vehement and tender (irascible and concupiscible), although between the two there are innumerable gradations. "Alterum (genus) quod Græci ἠθικόν vocant, ad naturas et ad mores et ad omnem vitæ consuetudinem accomodatum; alterum quod iidem παθητικόν nominant, quo perturbantur † animi et concitantur, in quo uno regnat

depends as much on the subjects to be treated of as on the character of the audience and the special aim of the speaker.

One field where pathetic eloquence once flourished is now almost barred to it, namely the Law Courts. True is it that in the procedure of the Courts speeches now and then occur, which are pervaded by strong feeling, but as a rule only in criminal cases and, rarely, in political tri. 's. In civil causes, on the other hand, pathos is deprecated, because, in disputes between two parties a clear understanding must be obtained by the judge of the question in dispute, and an impassioned address on it, which might influence him towards views otherwise than in accord with strict justice, would be considered offensive. In such a case, Eloquence must aim at giving a *thorough, precise, lucid* and, as far as possible, *attractive* presentation of the facts. Broeckaert, *Le Guide,* sec. 3, ch. 2.

* De Orat., 2, 51, 206. The Christian orator may excite love for good, aversion for evil; he may excite the emotions but not the passions in the bad sense of the word; these he must withstand. Always discriminating the person and the thing he must hate evil, while retaining his love for his fellowmen. In the study of the classics and, therefore, also in the examples therefrom given in this work, these principles must be most carefully kept in view as, in their more emotional passages, the ancients seldom (as unfortunately also many profane orators of modern times) rise to the level of the Christian standpoint.

† The use of the expression "perturbare animos" (stirring up of the soul) in the older Rhetoricians, comes from the stoic school, according to which πάθος =ταραχή, perturbatio (Zeno). This one-sided and exaggerated interpretation differs entirely from that of Aristotle (2, 1, and Ethics 1, 2), according to whom "perturbare animos" is only a metaphor, and a very poorly chosen one

oratio. Illud superius come, jucundum ad benevolentiam conciliandum paratum: hoc vehemens, incensum, incitatum, quo causæ eripiuntur."*

As a rule both kinds are found in conjunction. "Neque est ulla temperatior oratio quam illa in qua asperitas contentionis oratoris ipsius humanitate conditur: remissio autem lenitatis quadam gravitate et contentione firmatur."†

What are known as restrained passions are merely the expression of the oratorical methods (ἦθος) already mentioned.‡

Another distinction between direct and indirect pathos will be touched upon below.§

Third Article. *Choice of the Passions*

42. The selection, as well as the degree of the same, is determined by:

(1) The *object* of the speech. Every theme does not demand, nor can it support, strong emotions.

"Equidem primum considerare soleo, postuletne causa. Nam neque parvis in rebus adhibendæ sunt hæ dicendi faces, neque ita animatis hominibus, ut nihil ad eorum mentes oratione flectendas proficere possimus, ne aut irrisione, aut odio digni putemur, si aut tragœdias agamus in nugis, aut convellere adoriamur ea, quæ non possint commoveri."‖ "In parvis quidem litibus has tragœdias movere, tale est quale si personam Herculis et cothurnos aptare infantibus velis."¶

Theodoros** calls these rhetorical fantasies foolish bom-

---

at that. In contradiction to himself (12, 1) Quintilian says: "Ubi animis judicum vis afferenda est, et ab ipsa veri contemplatione abducenda mens; ibi proprium oratoris opus est"(6, 2, 5). A little before, however, he has: "Necessarios affectus fatebuntur, si aliter obtineri vera et justa et in commune profutura non possint" (6, 1, 7).

* Orat. c. 37, 128. † De Orat. 2, 53, 212.

‡ Cf. Quint. 6, 2, 8 sq.; Cic., De Orat. 2, 43. Yet ἦθος and restrained emotion are not identical; the latter is often a part of the former.

§ See 44, 1.

‖ "The first thing to consider is whether the cause requires that the minds of the audience should be excited, for such fiery oratory is not to be diverted to trivial subjects, nor when the minds of men are so affected that we can do nothing by eloquence to influence their opinions, lest we be thought to deserve ridicule or dislike, if we either act tragedies about trifles or endeavour to pluck up what cannot be moved."—De Orat. 2, 51, 205.

¶ Quint., Inst. vi. 1, 36. ** Of the Sublime, 3, 5.

bast—παρένθυρσος (frenzy)—and Martial, in his famous
Non de vi neque cæde, has made them thoroughly ridiculous.
While, however, irrelevant emotion is discouraged, no plea
is made for meagreness and dryness. Life, warmth and
thorough conviction ought to penetrate every speech which
is not a purely academic discourse.

(2) The *talent* and *character* of the orator. The first condition is that the emotion be true to nature. One must
not expect to soar at the beginning. "Illud præcipue
monendum, ne quis nisi summi ingenii viribus ad movendas
lacrymas aggredi audeat; nam ut est longe vehementissimus
hic, quum invaluit, affectus, ita, si nihil efficit, tepet; quam
melius infirmus actor tacitis judicum cogitationibus reliquis-
set. . . . *Nihil habet ista res medium, sed aut lacrimas meretur
aut risum.*"*

Every nature is responsive to a distinct set of emotions.
One orator feels himself more easily attracted to tender,
touching emotions, another to the vehement kind. If an orator wishes to impress his hearers, let him in this matter follow his own impulses and allow his own nature to speak and
act. Eloquence, that is, the Power of Passion, is subjective:
"Pectus est quod disertos facit"; but one's own heart must
urge, and not a pathos which has been, as it were, forced
into it. The universal *mind* is rarer, perhaps, than the universal *soul*. Kindly natures are not always gifted with the
power of moving others strongly and vice versa.

Again, in the employment of the emotions, the status and
dignity of the orator must be taken into consideration. There
are, for example, certain vehement emotions which would
appear less becoming in a person of high position than a
quiet, forcible manner of speaking. With reference to this a
humorous French proverb runs: "La dignité n'a pas de bras."

(3) *The Audience.* The particular emotions to be excited
must depend upon the character, disposition, rank and age
of the audience.†

---

* Quint., Inst. 6, 1, 44-45.

† In this respect, Aristotle gives further hints by means of his above-men-
tioned intellectual character paintings, which, in conjunction with his treatise
on the passions, are considered the golden part of his rhetoric.

ELOQUENCE

In his defence of Ligarius Cicero would have become an object of ridicule to Cæsar if he had given rein to excessive emotion, whereas he triumphed over him by his apparently contemptuous manner. One mood is adapted for passionate, another for cool, calculating natures; one for the masses, another for persons of dignity and education; one for the vivacious temperaments of the South, another for the stolid inhabitants of the North. For certain minds violent emotion is an imperative need if they are to be moved to a determination or to take some important step; in the case of others it is a kind of thunder-clap, stunning and frightening them, in some cases even doing grave harm; others, again, it only incites to ridicule.

Fourth Article. *Management of the Passions*

(a) *Emotion in the Orator*

43. If the orator wishes to lay hold of the feelings of his audience it is essential that *he himself* be *intensely affected*. "Summa circa movendos affectus in hoc posita est, ut moveamur ipsi";* or, as the poet says:

> Si vis me flere, dolendum est
> Primum ipsi tibi.†

"Ut enim nulla materies tam facilis ad exardescendum est, quæ nisi admoto igni ignem concipere possit: sic nulla mens est tam ad comprehendendam vim orationis parata, quæ possit incendi, nisi inflammatus ipse ad eam et ardens accesseris."‡

---

* Quint., Inst. 6, 2, 26.   † Hor., Ars Poet. 102-3.

‡ De Orat. 2, 45, 190. The absence of emotion in the orator very often causes a want of conviction in the listener. Plutarch relates in his life of Demosthenes that a certain Athenian once begged the orator to appear for him in an action for a serious wrong he had suffered; the man, however, stated his case in so unemotional a manner that Demosthenes said: "The thing is not credible, no injury has been done to you." "What," shouted the man, growing very excited, "I was not injured, not abused? I speak an untruth?" "Good," said Demosthenes, "now your deposition is worthy of belief"; and he immediately took up the case. Cicero tells us of a similar case regarding Callidus, against whom he was speaking in the law courts. This man was complaining in an unemotional way that some one was plotting against his life; whereupon Cicero replied that the falsehood of his accusation was quite clear from the indifferent and casual manner in which he spoke. " Hoc ipsum posui pro argumento, quod ille . . . tam solute egisset, tam leniter, tam oscitanter. Tu

How is the orator to attain to this state of mind? By earnest and deep consideration of the matter in question and by a thorough grasp of the case in all its bearings.

Cicero instances the intensity of feeling displayed by actors on the stage when portraying the characters they represent.*

Quintilian says ot a vivid intuition—*visiones:* "Has quisque bene conceperit, is erit in affectibus potentissimus." He then gives a striking example: "Hominem occisum queror: non omnia, quæ in re presenti accidisse credibile est, in oculis habebo? non percussor ille subitus erumpet? non expavescet circumventus? exclamabit? vel rogabit vel fugiet? non ferientem, non concidentem videbo? non animo sanguis et pallor et gemitus, extremus denique expirantis hiatus insidet?" †

(b) *The Emotions : How the hearer should be prepared for their reception*

44. In many cases, spontaneous outbursts of emotion, flung suddenly at the audience, produce a much greater impression than those which are carefully worked up; thus we have the *exordium ex abrupto.* But such occasions are very rare; and when they occur, the outburst ought to be justified by the circumstances under pain of seeming out of place or even of making the speaker ridiculous. Hence Cicero gives us the following warning: "Non assiliendum statim est ad illud genus orationis."‡ "Qui non preparatis auribus inflammare rem cœpit, furere apud sanos et quasi inter sobrios bacchari vinolentus videtur."§

(1) The best way to prepare the mind of the listeners consists in the use of the so-called *Indirect Pathos.* When the emotion of the speaker pours out in an unrestrained and inevitable stream, it is called *direct* or fulminating pathos.

istuc, M. Callidi, nisi fingeres sic ageres? . . . ubi dolor? ubi ardor animi, qui etiam ex infantium ingeniis elicere voces et querelas solet? Nulla perturbatio animi, nulla corporis . . . itaque tantum abfuit, ut inflammares nostros animos; somnum isto loco vix tenebamus." Brut. 80, 277-278.

* De Orat. 2, 46, 193.

† Quint. 6, 2, 30, 31. See *illustration* or *picture-forming,* 38, 4.

‡ De Orat. 2, 53, 213.   § Orat. 28, 99.

Indirect pathos consists in the presentation of some thought, of some deed or historic passage, which, of itself, without any effort on the part of the speaker, lays hold of, touches and moves the heart of the listeners. Now it is merely a simple narration, now a lively, artistic description. The orator speaks rather as an impartial witness than as a man surrendering himself to the flood of feeling. For example, he describes the lot of some unfortunate man or the persecution of an innocent one, his quiet resignation, his humility amid all his woes; the simple relation arouses the same feeling of sorrow, compassion and indignation against injustice and tyranny, as direct pathos might have aroused, and, not infrequently, succeeds even better.* These same feelings may then be nourished and increased by direct *Pathos*.

The effect of indirect pathos often seems quite at variance with the cause; for example, the calmness of an innocent man in the midst of a great danger or in heartrending trouble, evokes in us by sympathy, emotions of anxiety, fear or horror.

Cicero prepares the minds of his listeners for the deep emotions he intends to call up on Milo's behalf by relating his conversations, his remarks with regard to his fate, and the happiness of his fellow townsmen; in his speech *de Suppliciis* he pictures to the judges the innocence of the ship captains, the youth of the majority of them, the unjust and cruel treatment which preceded their execution, the grief of their parents, etc., in order thereby to excite against Verres the most vehement feelings of anger and hatred.

Lally-Tollendal, after recounting the intrigues of his father's enemies, and the bitter complaints which the latter, after many vain efforts, had made to the King, as well as his fruitless appeals from his prison, continues: "Oh, where is there a being who would not be moved by the sight of a virtuous man, who from the depths of his prison is able to follow all the machinations of his enemies and yet can do

---

* Hence is explained the feeling of sympathy by which we are seized when reading or hearing read some affecting poem, or when present at the performance of some tragic scene. This is caused by means of the objective character of the circumstance.

nothing to frustrate them! Who can foresee all the terrible results and yet cannot take measures beforehand against them! Who can find no one, no one to whom he can turn for help! Who sees all means of defence, one after another, torn from his hands! Who only begs to enlighten his judges and may not! To whom not even the comfort of a quick death is vouchsafed; nay, according to the unjust sentence of a judge, burning with hatred, must he rather wait for a lingering death! A judge burning with hatred! Oh, to such a thought one cannot become accustomed—Hatred and a judge! Such a combination fills the soul with horror and stifles human speech!''

Indirect pathos serves not only *as a preparation* for the direct, it must often *entirely replace it;* indeed, there are circumstances when the orator, from considerations of prudence, must altogether renounce the expression of very strong emotions.

Any display of vehemence on the part of Shakespeare's Antony would most likely have still further angered and estranged those who were sharers in the murder of Cæsar, whereas the mere uncovering of the bloody corpse and reading of his will were quite sufficient to fill the people with indignation against the conspirators.

An ill-timed and immoderate outburst of emotion may lead to the embarrassment of the speaker.

(2) Another and very commendable manner of preparation for the emotions is the use of a *clear, searching* and *fervid argumentation.* While the heart influences the head, the head also reacts on the heart, and nothing is more calculated to stir both speaker and audience than a vigorous and triumphant array of proofs. Demosthenes employs this method, and, among pulpit orators, Bourdaloue.

(c) *Strengthening the Emotions: Their Duration*

45. (1) There are two modes *of strengthening the emotions: by joining together several emotions,* and by what is called *oratorical illustration.*

For the purpose of intensifying an emotion, the orator prepares the way by accentuating some other emotion, and often, if one may judge from appearances, one of a contrary nature; or several emotions are "heaped up," and the vehement, overpowering passion which results calls up in the heart a wealth of sensations of which some, by their relation to the previous emotion, or by contrast with it, serve as preparation or as fuel for a sympathy still more intense. The heart lays hold of certain emotions, or rather allows itself to be seized by them, only when it has already climbed to a certain height in the scale of feeling. Hatred and indignation, for example, burn much more fiercely when they are fanned by sarcasm; and these emotions are intensified by sympathy and love for those who appear as the opponents of all that is hateful, unjust or cruel.

Still this interaction of the passions is only a stage of the journey.

Cicero's *de Suppliciis* should be studied to learn what enormous influence the change of emotions exercises upon the heart, and with what a fund of knowledge of mankind Cicero understands how, by means of contrasts, to model according to circumstances and to bring to perfection this change. In this respect, especially, the passages relating to the victory of the pirates, the fate of the ship captains and their parents, and that about Gavius, are instructive examples. In the latter passage* Cicero arouses, first of all, sympathy. "Cædebatur virgis . . ."; and then his sympathy and sorrow break forth in the words: "O nomen dulce libertatis. . .", after which he excites indignation on account of the contempt displayed for the rights of Roman citizenship, and fear in the face of this common danger. "Quid enim nuper tu ipse. Homines tenues, obscuro loco nati. . . ." Anger, too, he arouses, over the enormity of the offence: "Facinus est, vinciri civem Romanum . . .", then he passes back to sympathy: "Sic hæc non ad cives Romanos. . . Paullo ante, judices, lacrimas in morte misera . . ." See the passage in Appendix III, 3; also Cicero's peroration in *pro Milone*, his speeches *pro Flacco, Plancio, Sulla, Murena;* and Lord Chatham's Speech against the American War.

* c. 62.

MEANS: THE EMOTIONS

Oratorical illustration, already touched upon,* appears now in short passages, now in prolonged descriptions, according to the object in view.†

Cicero affords us many examples in the speech against Verres. He pictures very vividly the cruelty of Verres towards Gavius. "Ipse inflammatus scelere et furore in forum venit . . . Cædebatur virgis in medio foro Messanæ civis Romanus. . . . "‡

In the same way he introduces to the judge the parents and relations of the unhappy ship captains, and pictures the mourning of the survivors: §

"Behold, behold, gentlemen, the miserable and squalid condition of our allies. Sthenius, the Thermitan, whom you see here, with hair dishevelled and in mourning, though his whole house has been stripped of everything, makes no mention of your robberies (O Verres); his own safety, himself alone he claims from you. For you, by your lust and wickedness, have driven him from his country, where he occupied the position of a leading man, gained by his many virtues and distinguished services. This man Dexius here, demands of you not the public treasures stripped from Tyndaris, nor his own private wealth, of which you robbed him, but wretched man that he is, his only son, his most virtuous and innocent boy. . . . This other man here, the aged Eubulida, has not, at his advanced time of life, undertaken such a long and fatiguing journey to recover any of his property, but to see you condemned with those eyes that beheld the bleeding neck of his own son. Had Lucius Metellus allowed it, gentlemen, the mothers of these men, their wives and sisters would be on their way hither; and one of them, with all the matrons of Heraclea, as I approached that city late at night, came to meet me with many torches; and styling me her saviour, you her executioner, calling on the name of her son, the wretched woman cast herself at my feet, as if I were able to raise her boy from death. In the other cities, too, the aged mothers and even the little children and wretched men did the same; while

* 38, 4.   † Cf. also No. 123 below.   ‡ c. 62.   § 48, 128.

77

the helpless age of each class kept claiming my labour and care, and your good faith and pity."

In the peroration to *Pro Fonteio* Cicero causes the sister (a Vestal Virgin) of the accused to appear: "Tendit ad vos virgo vestalis manus supplices, easdem quas pro vobis deis immortalibus tendere consuevit . . ."*

Cœnus wishing to induce Alexander to march back to Macedonia, draws a harrowing description of the miserable state of the army; he says, "Behold our wasted bodies pierced by so many wounds and seared by scars! Our swords are all but blunt, our armour almost falling to pieces! Who is there that has still a coat of mail or a horse? We have conquered all, and yet we are in need of all things."†

Hugh Blair on the subject of Oratorical Illustration says: "This must be the style of the orator when he would be pathetic; and this will be the style if he speaks from real feeling; bold, ardent, simple. No sort of description will succeed, but what is written *fervente calamo*. If he stay until he can work up his style, and finish and adorn it, he will infallibly cool his own ardour; and then he will touch the heart no more. His composition will become frigid, it will be the language of one who describes, but who does not feel. We must take notice that there is a great difference between appealing to the imagination and appealing to the heart. The former may be done coolly and at leisure, the latter must always be rapid and ardent. In the former, art and labour may be suffered to appear; in the latter, no effect can follow, unless it seems to be the work of nature only."‡

46. *With regard to the duration of the Passions*, it is to be remarked in general that the orator must let himself be guided by the dictates of his own heart; he must never continue to draw artificially on the same passion, when its source in the feeling is beginning to dry up; this takes place in the hearer much earlier than in the speaker. The stronger the emotions, the sooner they are exhausted. "Nunquam debet

---

* 21, 46.   † Curt. 9, 3, 10.
‡ Hugh Blair, *Lectures on Rhetoric*, xxxii.

esse longa miseratio [the same holds good of every other feeling]; nec sine causa dictum est: nihil facilius quam lacrymas inarescere."*

But, at the same time, if the pathetic outburst is not to be prolonged neither must it be too suddenly broken off. In this case again nature must be the guide. After a passage of strong emotion the normal state should be regained, not of a sudden, not as it were, with a bound, but little by little, step by step. Nothing shows more clearly that an emotion is not real, but only artificial and feigned, than when the orator, almost in the same breath, speaks as quietly and calmly as though there had not been the slightest change in his inmost feelings. By doing this he makes as strange an impression as the orator who introduces into his speech witty remarks, demonstrations of learning, etc.

Are emotions, which resemble shooting stars, in that they burst suddenly into view and as quickly die away, allowable in a speech? Certainly. In the right place they are an effective means of enlivening a narrative or proof, or of concluding in a forcible manner. But they must be quite natural, spring from the heart, and *not* be the product of any artificial manufacture.

In reply to the complaint of the Emperor Titus, "I have lost a day; because to-day I have not conferred a benefit on anyone," Thomas bursts forth, "What sayest thou, great Prince? That is not true; no, for this day, on which thou hast uttered these words, shall be an everlasting example to kings; this day cannot be lost to thy honour, for never hast thou been greater, never more beneficent to humanity!†

Lally-Tollendal closes the narrative of the tragic death of his father with these words, "O my father! if thou hast bequeathed to me fearful sorrows and heavy responsibilities, also hast thou left me an example of sublime virtues! Thy courage must strengthen mine, so that death a thousand times over shall not terrify me from raising my voice against injustice. All France shall ring with the wail of my grief; I will force my way to the very throne, I will embrace the feet of the glorious monarch, by whose side sits immaculate justice; I will cry out, "Sire, mercy and justice! Mercy for an

---

*Inst. 6, 1.   † Essai sur des Éloges, iii, 21.

unhappy man, who is obliged to appeal against the first court of the Empire! Justice for a virtuous man, who in the very heart of this Empire fell a victim to calumny!"

In great orators we sometimes find transitions enlivened and elevated by means of a strong burst of emotion, and this chiefly in pulpit oratory; e.g., in Massillon and Bossuet the outward form is in these cases usually disguised under some rhetorical figure of speech.

(d) *Overcoming an emotion in the hearer which is not favourable to the Orator.*

47. The speaker is sometimes called upon to overcome, or at least to fight and reduce, a prejudice which exists in the mind of the audience. This is usually very difficult, and requires the employment of all the orator's skill and knowledge of human nature. An emotion may be combatted either directly or indirectly.

(i) *Directly. By endeavouring to remove an emotion by substituting its opposite*: "ut odio benevolentia, misericordia invidia tollatur."*

Thus Demosthenes shows that Midias, instead of deserving sympathy by his tears, was rather deserving of contempt and hatred by his impudence. So, too, in the speech touched upon above † did Capitolinus excite the agitation and animosity of the Roman people by the confession of his disgrace, when he thought to arouse thereby sympathy and compassion.

But often the prejudice is only increased if attacked suddenly and with violence, so that the orator inspires only aversion or even disgust. How could a person, for example, who is in great grief on account of some recent misfortune, be expected to lay aside at command all his sorrowful feelings?

2. *Indirectly. By opposing to the excitement of the hearer coolness and the quiet language of reason.*

Cæsar takes this line in speaking to the Senators incensed against the supporters of Catiline. He leads them to consider those qualities which statesmen who are about to treat upon important matters should possess: "Omnes homines, P. C.,

---

* De Orat. 2, 53, 216. † 37.

qui de rebus dubiis consultant, ab odio, amicitia, ira atque misericordia vacuos esse decet."*

Cicero, on the other hand, in order effectively to counter-act the unemotional, apathetic state of mind induced by Cæsar, purposely paints a strong and vivid picture of the fearful dangers that would have swept over their country with the success of Catiline's conspiracy.†

The emotions should abate as soon as the orator has suc-ceeded in destroying the foundations (or causes) upon which they rest.

Moreover, in this and in other cases in order not to make a false step one must credit the hearer with the manifold good qualities in his disposition (see below figure of speech —Concession) make use of language, which, although always calm and collected must never be frigid and indifferent; he must use conciliatory expressions, and endeavour, by avoiding everything which may excite the imagination and feelings, to lead the hearer to a thoughtful consideration and appraisement of the object of his prejudice.

(ii) *By distracting the thoughts*, that is by guiding the mind of the listeners and attracting their attention to something entirely different and, if possible, more important.

Demosthenes in his speech for Diopithes or that about the Chersonese, at first draws the attention of his hearers com-pletely away from the affairs of Diopithes against whom they were prejudiced; he treats of the threatening state of the Republic with which he connects the concerns of Dio-pithes, and shows that his army ought to be kept up and the man himself in consequence rather supported than punished; by this means he increases, in a very marked degree, the indignation of the audience against Philip and his supporters, and also against the accusers of Diopithes. Similar in this respect is the entire speech of Cicero's *Pro Ligario*, the speeches of Demosthenes for the Inhabitants of Megalopolis, in which he opposes their prejudices most tactfully and circumspectly, and that on the Freedom of the Inhabitants of Rhodes, in which against the dislike settled in the minds of his hearers he sets off the nobility and dignity

* De Conj. Cat. c. 51.　　† 4 Cat.

of generosity; finally, the masterly speeches of Pacuvius in defence of Perolla and of Veturia to Coriolanus. But the most noteworthy example is offered by the elevated sentiments embodied in the celebrated speech of Flavius to Theodosius.*

(iii) By *treating* the emotion in a *happy vein of raillery* or *irony*, though care must be taken not to offend the prejudices of the audience. "Rerum sæpe maximarum momenta vertit (risus) ut cum odium viamque frequentissime frangat." † The when and how is not bound by rules. Tact and good sense must serve in this as in other cases, as the surest guiding stars; it may, however, be remarked that joking and irony are scarcely ever employed in pulpit oratory; only perhaps when the objections of bombastic unbelievers need it, or in the case of certain crimes, which call for sharper weapons to secure their condemnation.

Cicero wishes to discount the circumstance that Clodius was murdered in the Appian Way (which had been constructed by an ancestor of Clodius). He says: "Of course the death of P. Clodius is a much more shocking affair, since he was killed among the tombs of his ancestors! This is the plea oft put forward by the plaintiffs, as if old Appius Cœcus had built the road, not for public use, but that his descendants might carry out their rascally designs with impunity. So when that most accomplished Roman gentleman, Marcus Papirius, fell a victim on that same Appian Way to the hand of P. Clodius, the crime, forsooth, was to go unpunished. But now, on this occasion, what a cloud of tragedy hangs over that same Appian Way! When it was dyed with the blood of an honourable and innocent man, not a word was said, but since it has been stained with the blood of a robber and a parricide, everybody is talking about it."‡

In another passage Cicero used a strong burst of emotion for the same object.§

§ 2. *Of the Passions taken singly*

First Article. *Excitement of Particular Emotions*

48. The tactful employment of the passions is of the first importance, but as it presents many difficulties, which can

---

* See Appendix xxii.   † Quint. Inst. 6, 3, 9.
‡ Pro Milo. 7, 17.   § Cf. also Pro Milo. 33, 90.

only be surmounted by the study of numerous examples, we put before the aspiring orator a selection which should prove not only useful but fascinating, inasmuch as some of the most beautiful features of eloquence are to be met with in the domain of the emotions.*

(a) Emotions which arise out of the idea of some good.

(i) *Love. Admiration. Gratitude.*

(i) *Love.*

– 49 *Love.* The orator endeavours (1) to gain the love of his hearers for *himself* by convincing them of his love for them, his zeal for their interests, his desire for self-sacrifice. (2) The love for *another personality* will be aroused most easily by displaying the transcendant qualities, the merits and the virtues of that person; as innocence in the case of children and the unhappy, modesty, generosity, sense of charity, mildness and kindness. "Quam illa † ardentes amores excitaret sui, si videretur!" We are drawn to love others by kinship, by their connexion with those we love already, by similarity of tastes or character, and above all by the knowledge that we are ourselves objects of affection. Love begets a return of love.‡ (3) The love of a *quality* or *object* (e.g., of a particular virtue, of a profession, of an undertaking) is called into being by means of a vigorous exposition of (a) its excellence (grandeur, nobility, stateliness, beauty); (b) the great utility and happiness we hope to obtain from it for ourselves or for others who are dear to us.

Cicero works upon the affections of the Romans, by speaking to them of his love for them and for their country.

"Shall I not be solicitous for my fellow-citizens? Shall not all my thoughts, night and day, be devoted to the service of the State? For, do I not owe you everything, Quirites? I, a man without famous ancestors? I, whom you have preferred

* Aristotle investigates in respect to every emotion the following four points: (a) Who is especially inclined towards it? (b) Against whom is it directed? (c) From what cause does it spring? (d) Employment of the particular points of view for the oratorical excitement of the passions. Cf. also Cicero, De Orat 2, 51-52.

† Namely *sapientia,* φρόνησις, wisdom according to the teaching of Socrates is the foundation of all virtues. See Cicero, de Fin. 2, 16, 52, and Plato, Phædr. 250 D. (c. 31).

‡ Cf. the two motives of love which Aristotle (Rhet. 2, 4) enumerates.

to more celebrated men? ... Therefore, Quirites, I will
serve you with all the powers of my soul; and with work,
even above my strength, I will keep ward and watch for you.
How could a citizen, especially one holding the position I
hold, be so unmindful of your goodness, so estranged from
his country, as not to be filled with gratitude on account of
your benefits?" *

A similar passage is found in Cicero's 4 Cat. 1, 1-2. "I
see," etc. Other examples of this emotion are found in the
perorations of *Pro Flacco* and *Pro Plancio;* in that of *Pro
Milone,* in which he, in order to fill the judges with sympathy
for Milo, makes much of his fortitude, his benefits to his
country, his love of his fellow-citizens: "Nolite, si in nostro
omnium fletu nullam lacrimam aspexistis Milonis. ..."
Then he pictures his own love for Milo, the sorrow which
he, Cicero, and his will feel if Milo is not declared innocent:
"Hæc tu mecum sæpe his absentibus" ... and after he has
implored the judges and the troops to espouse Milo's cause
he proceeds: "Quid? vos judices? ... Vos, vos appello, for-
tissimi viri. ... Quodnam ego concepi tantum scelus?" ...
Finally he supplicates all creation, gods, judges, country,
for his client, and does not restrain even his tears.

Related to love is *Admiration.* The more strongly this is
dwelt upon, or the more pertinently the distinctive traits of a
person or an action are depicted, the more surely is it excited.

Pliny's panegyric on Cicero runs: "How could I in
justice pass you over, O Marcus Tullius? Which of your
glorious crowns of honour shall I single out? What can be
more worthy of special distinction than the unanimous testimony of the Roman people as to the nobility of your life,
which reached the culminating point during your consulship?
At your word the tribes gave up their claim to the Agrarian
Law, the very food of their life; ... your eloquence induced
the sons of the nobility to consider office-hunting disgraceful;
your genius drove Catiline to take to flight, and Marcus
Antonius into banishment. Hail to you, the first to be called
Father of your country, the first to celebrate a triumph in
the toga! whose eloquence gained the laurel wreath, who

* 6 Phil. 6, 17 and 7, 18.

became the father of Roman knowledge! Truly did Cæsar, once your enemy, write of you that your laurels overshadowed all triumphs; for it is greater deed to have increased the domain of the Roman mind than that of the Roman Empire!"*

Cicero kindles the passion of admiration in the hearts of the Romans for Pompey † by extolling in terms of glorious exaggeration his great qualities.

A similar line must be taken in order to rouse up the emotion of *gratitude*: ‡

For this purpose (a) the *magnitude* of the benefit received must be demonstrated; how much we need it, and what happy results it will have for us; (b) *the noble intention*, the benevolence and magnanimity of the giver must also be emphasized; the benefit was not deserved on our part, perhaps we were not worthy of it; (c) *the circumstances* attendant upon the gift; perhaps the benefactor deprived himself of some possession, or he gave only with inconvenience and sacrifice; or mayhap the circumstance called for even greater commendation on account of the high dignity of the giver. Cicero affords an example of this in III Cat. C. 8, when he calls upon all to return thanks to the gods.

The most beautiful expression and the most sublime subjects of this emotion are found in pulpit oratory. Inspired by heavenly desire St Chrysostom cries:

"If the choice were given me between sitting in glory with the angels or by the side of Paul in prison, I would choose the latter. If Christ Himself for my sake became man, stripped Himself of His glory, and chose rather to be crucified for me than to be honoured, shall not I be prepared to suffer all joyfully for His sake? Listen to His words: 'Father, glorify Thy Son!' O my Redeemer! Thou sufferest Thyself to be nailed to the cross, to die the death of a malefactor with robbers and murderers! Thou allowest Thy sacred face to be spat upon, to be struck; and this Thou callest glorification! Yes, all this I bear for those I love, and look upon it as glory! If He who loved the miserable and the wretched, called the disgrace borne for us glory, and not

* Pliny, Hist. Nat. 7, 31.   † Pro Lege Manilia, c. 10.
‡ Cf. Arist. 2, 7 : Περὶ τοῦ χαρίζεσθαι καὶ ἀχαριστεῖν.

that which was derived from His Father, should not I, therefore, consider it a much greater honour! O blessed bonds, O holy hands, ornamented with such chains! The hands of Paul, when he cured the lame man and caused him to walk, were not so worthy of veneration as when they were bound with chains. Had I been alive in those times, with reverence would I have embraced them and touched my eyes with them; I would never have tired of kissing those hands which had been manacled for the sake of my Lord!"*

And St Bernard, glowing with charity arising from the love of his Saviour, bursts forth:

"What return shall I make to the Lord for all He has done for me? If all the lives of the sons of Adam, all the days of the world and the deeds of all mankind, which were, are and ever will be, were given to me, all would be as nothing in comparison with that Body sacrificed for us, wonderful and glorious on account of its heavenly gifts, in the conception by the Holy Ghost, the being born of a Virgin, the innocence of its life, the fulfilment of the Scriptures, the glory of miracles, the discovery of secrets! As far as the heavens are above the earth, so is that Life above ours, and yet it was offered for our salvation! Just as 'nothingness' cannot be compared with infinity, neither can our lives be compared with the life of the Saviour, for nothing could be more sublime than the latter, nothing meaner than the former. Think not that I exaggerate, for no words can tell, no eye can see the secret of such humiliation. If I were to give Him all I have, all I am capable of, would it not be merely what a star is to the sun, a speck of dust to a mountain, a barley-corn to a stack? I have but two mites, body and soul, or rather only one, my *will;* and shall I not give it to Him, who, so great of Himself, has enriched a miserable creature such as I with immeasurable benefits, and who, at the price of His whole Being, has ransomed me? But if I am determined to keep my will for myself, with what assurance, with what countenance, with what intention, with what knowledge, could I appear before the infinite mercy of God, and dare to break down that strong bulwark which protected Israel, and claim as my pro-

*8 Hom. on the Epistle to the Ephesians.

tection, not drops, nay streams of blood, which gush forth from the five wounds of His sacred body?"*

(ii) *Desire*

50. This emotion is excited in the same way as love. Particularly effective is a lively picturing of the *happiness* that we should enjoy if the object of our desire were in our possession; the *honour* which would accrue to us therefrom, the *moral advantage* of having it. The emotion of desire will be measurably increased by the excitement of its antithesis, e.g., the need in which we should find ourselves without the object of our desire; the *danger* we might be subject to.

Alexander wishes to inspire his soldiers with such enthusiasm that they will clamour to follow him still further: He says: "I lead you rather to Booty than to Glory; you are deserving of carrying back to your country those treasures which the sea bears to the coast; you are the men to leave no stone unturned, to be stopped by no dangers. Therefore I pray you by your fame, which is superior to all moral fame; I pray you by my services to you and yours to me—wherein we have emulated each other—I pray and conjure you, now when I am near the summit of success, not to forsake your foster-brother, much less your king!"†

An affecting expression of desire is the celebrated complaint of Electra in Sophocles; the letter of the holy martyr Ignatius to the Christians of Rome is an heroic expression of the same emotion.

(iii) *Joy*

51. This grows out of the possession of some good and is aroused by describing (1) how *great*, (2) how *unexpected* or even how *long expected* and vouchsafed to few, (3) how *sure* the benefit in question is. This emotion requires in its development *liveliness*, in its delivery *cheerfulness of mien*. It occurs especially in the occasional address.

The exordium of the Second Catiline speech ‡ is the expression of Cicero's radiant delight and an invitation to all to rejoice because of the departure of Catiline from Rome:

* Serm. de Quadruplici Debito. cf. also Salvian, De Gubernat. 4, 10.
† Curt. 9, 2, 27. Cf. also Cicero, Pro Domo sua, 37, 100. "Sin mea domus," etc.
‡ 1, 1.

"Tandem aliquando, Quirites ... forasque projecerit." Cicero also gives utterance to the same emotion in presence of the Roman people after his return: "Nothing is more desired by man than an equable and enduring prosperity, an undisturbed and cheerful career; and yet, had the course of my life remained untroubled, I should never have known the indescribable, nay, even god-like rapture, which has become mine through your goodness.... O ye immortal gods! is not one's native land dear and lovable above all? How glorious a view is furnished by our Italy! How teeming with people its towns! How splendid its landscapes! its meadows! its productions! What a magnificent capital! how its citizens excel in culture! how glorious is the State on account of its dignity, and you by your majesty! All these privileges did I enjoy more than anyone!" etc.*

(iv) *Hope*

52. Hope is the expectation of some benefit.† It includes the feeling of desire; it also presupposes the power of attaining the said benefit and hence joins also with the desire *confidence* of victoriously overcoming the difficulties which stand in the way of the fulfilment of the same (*spes=desiderium fiduciale*). The fruit of hope is *courage* and *boldness*. Since the strength and liveliness of hope are in proportion to the nature of the benefit, the means for attaining it, and its nearness or remoteness, so in order to arouse and enhance this emotion, it must be shown: (1) How great, glorious and enduring the hope for the *benefit* in question is; (2) How reliable the *means* for its attainment are; (3) How *soon* it may be attained.

For the development of these grounds for hope the following points may be of use: the promise, the good will, the power and good faith of the person from whom we expect it; what personal strength and means are at our disposition, or what assistance is offered us by God, by friends or by cir-

---

* Ad. Quint. post red, 1, 2. See also Cicero in Pis. 22, 52, "Unus ille dies. . . . " St Leo also calls up this feeling in his Sermon de Nat. Dom., "Salvator noster;" St Chrysostom, Hom. 21 de statuis (Pardoning of Antioch); St Bernard, Serm. de S. Victore, and Serm. 1 in vig. Nat. Dom.

† Cic. Tusc. 4, 37, 80.

cumstances; how many, and perhaps how often, others have already asked for this benefit; how small are the obstacles; how trifling the power and the efforts of opponents. *Courage* and *boldness* are excited by showing: how great is the object of an undertaking, how beautiful, useful, necessary; how commendable its accomplishment; how entirely feasible it is, how, already, greater obstacles have been overcome.*

Alexander says to his soldiers: "We have only a march of four days before us, we, who have crossed so many snowy plains, so many rivers, so many mountains. No longer does that sea, which barred our way with its waters, hinder us, no longer do the defiles of Cilicia stop our way, all lies before us free and open; we stand on the threshold of victory, merely a few deserters and murderers of their master remain. In truth a glorious work, which shall be counted among the foremost of your deeds and will hand you down to the admiration of posterity."

Compare with this General Wolfe's address to his soldiers before Quebec:

"I congratulate you, my brave countrymen and fellow-soldiers, on the spirit and success with which you have executed this important part of our enterprise. The formidable Heights of Abraham are now surmounted, and the city of Quebec, the object of all our toils, now stands in view of us. A perfidious enemy, who have dared to exasperate you by their cruelties but not to oppose you on equal ground, are now constrained to face you on the open plain, without ramparts or intrenchments to shelter them.

"You know too well the forces which compose their army to dread their superior numbers. A few regular troops from old France, weakened by hunger and sickness, who, when fresh, were unable to withstand British soldiers, are their general's chief dependence. Those numerous companies of Canadians, insolent, mutinous, unsteady and ill-disciplined, have exercised his utmost skill to keep them together to this time; and as soon as their irregular ardour is damped by our firm fire, they will instantly turn their backs and give you no further trouble but in the pursuit. As for those savage

* Cf. Arist. 2, 11.

tribes of Indians, whose horrid yells in the forest have struck many a bold heart with affright, terrible as they are with the tomahawk and scalping-knife to a flying and prostrate foe, you have experienced how little their ferocity is to be dreaded by resolute men upon fair and open ground; you will now only consider them as the objects of a severe revenge for the unhappy fate of many slaughtered countrymen.

"This day puts it into your power to terminate the fatigues of a siege, which has so long employed your courage and patience. Possessed with a full confidence of the certain success which British valour must gain over such enemies, I have led you up these steep and dangerous rocks, only solicitous to show you the foe within your reach. The impossibility of a retreat makes no difference in the situation of men resolved to conquer or die: and believe me, my friends, if your conquest could be bought with the blood of your general, he would most cheerfully resign a life which he has long devoted to his country."

Demosthenes frequently enkindles hope in the hearts of the Athenians, and usually joins with it blame for their negligence and also its antithesis, fear, on account of their frivolity. Cf. I Phil. 4-9: Εἰ δέ τις ὑμῶν, ὦ ἄ. Ἀθ., δυσπολέμητον οἴεται τὸν Φίλιππον . . . , and especially the passage in the Second Olynthiacs, in which he shows that Philip's power, founded as it was on deceit and injustice, could not be durable, and how the Athenians, through their own efforts, could recover what they had lost.

Equally as powerful is the emotion of hope in the speeches of O'Connell to the people. This emotion, however, is most beautifully displayed in spiritual eloquence. Compare the passage in St Bernard, where he exhorts to confidence in Mary,* and that in St Chrysostom, where he exhorts us to hope in the mercy of God.†

(v) *Emulation* ‡

53. In order to stimulate emulation, (1) an *object worthy* of *striving* for as virtue, wisdom, eloquence, bravery, respect

---

* Hom. 2, super Missus est and in Nativ. B.M.V.
† Hom. 8 de Pœnitentia; Hom. 2 in Ps. 50; Paraenes. ad Theod., etc.
‡ Aristot. Rhet. 2, 11.

for superiors, must be placed before the mind, and (2) the *persons* who are distinguished, and whom he must emulate, must be pointed out: these are ancestors, fellow-countrymen, relations, friends, men of a like age and calling. Analogy may be very advantageously employed by showing that those, whose example is to urge us on, were in similar circumstances (position, age, resources, fate), that they had to struggle with the same or greater difficulties, that they earned the thanks and admiration of their country. . . . Frequently the Comparatio a minori ad majus comes in.

In many parts of his speech *pro Sestio** Cicero arouses in the Roman youth the feeling of noble endeavour and emulation: "Imitate those men, I beg you, in the name of the immortal gods, you who seek for dignity and praise and glory. These examples are honourable, godlike, immortal; they are celebrated by fame, and are committed to the eternal recollection of our annals and are handed down to posterity. It is a labour, I do not deny; great is the danger, I admit it:

> The path of virtue is beset with snares!

A very true saying; still,

> To covet that which many envy, many desire, and yet to whom the toil involved in their attainment, is foolish.†

"Therefore let us imitate our Bruti, our Camilli and Ahalæ our Decii, our Curii and Fabricii and Maximi, our Scipios our Lentuli, our Æmilii and countless others who have given liberty to this republic. Let us love our country; let us obey the Senate; let us consult the interests of the good; let us disregard present rewards and fix our eyes on the glory which we shall receive from posterity."

Read also in Livy speech of Appius to the Roman people: "Obsecro vos, venandi studium . . ."; ‡ in Curtius the speech of Alexander to his friends, "Ego vero non deero. . . ."§ St Eucharius exhorts his hearers to imitate the saints in the following words: "O ye who contemplate the trials of the saints, why do ye not also think of their heavenly crowns?

---

* Pro Sestio, 48, 102 ; 68, 143. Cf. also 65, 136 sqq.; also I Phil. 14, 34, and Pro Lege Man. 4, 11.

† From the tragedy "Thyestes," by the Roman Poet, Attius.

‡ 5, 69.   § 9, 6, 21.

Consider how the sufferings of the saints and martyrs in all times made the path to glory; death was only a stepping-stone to happiness, and by closing the gate of this earthly life, that of eternal felicity was opened; fortitude in suffering, which the world despised, gained heaven. Patience is the sublime example which Divine Providence puts before the eyes of the human race."*

II. *Emotions which arise out of the Idea of some Evil*

(i) *Hatred*

54. This is aroused by the description of the repellant features of some object, e.g., of a vice, by showing how despicable, disgraceful, dangerous and destructive it is. The picture, however, must not be *devoid of dignity* nor contrary to truth or Christian charity, and so must be applied only to things, never to persons.

How Cicero was accustomed to make use of this passion we can judge from the following example; he wishes to arouse hatred against Antonius's methods: "Quid hic faciet, si poterit, iratus, qui quum succensere nemini posset, omnibus bonis fuerit inimicus? quid hic victor non audebit, qui nullam adeptus victoriam, tanta scelera post Caesaris interitum fecerit? refertam ejus domum exhauserit? hortos compilarit?"†

By picturing the haughtiness of the Romans, the leader, Pontius, kindles in his soldiers the feeling of hatred against that nation. "For what more could have been done to propitiate heaven and to pacify man than we have done? The possessions of the enemy, taken as spoils of war, which by the laws of war appeared to be ours, we have restored; those who were responsible for hostilities we have surrendered—dead, because alive was an impossibility; their goods, that no guilt might linger among us from contact with them, we have carried to Rome. What further debt do I owe you, Romans? What more do I owe to the treaty, or to the gods that witnessed it? Whom shall I propose to decide the question of your wrath and of my punishment? I decline none, be the judge an individual or a community. If, however, the

*Hom. de SS. MM. Epiphod. et Alex. † 3 Phil. 12, 30.

and yet you attack him, whom you cannot fear and ought not to hate, and when you see he has nothing left which you can take away from him, unless you are indignant at this, that you see him sitting with his clothes on in this court whom you turned naked out of his patrimony as if off a wreck?* In *Pro Domo sua*, 23, 59, he reproaches his enemies with their injustice: "Quid enim vos uxor mea misera violarat, quam vexavistis, raptavistis, omni, crudelitate lacerastis? Quid? mea filia—quid parvus filius—quid frater meus?" Cf. "Hanc tætram immanemque belluam, vinctam auspiciis . . .";† also *De Suppl.* (c. 32), in which Cicero is indignant because a Syracusan, Kleomenes, commanded the Roman warships; also *Pro Quinctio* (c. 18), against Nævius; *in Vatin* (8, 19). Cf. St Chrysost., Hom. 21 in 1 Cor. on uncharitableness to the poor.

When Lord Suffolk, in the British Parliament, expressed the opinion that every kind of treatment was justifiable against the American insurgents, and that ministers were fully warranted in making use of all the means God and nature had put into their hands, the Earl of Chatham, burning with indignation against such opinions, cried out: "My Lords, these enormities cry aloud for redress and punishment. But this barbarous measure has been defended, not only on the principles of policy and necessity, but also on those of morality; 'for it is perfectly allowable,' says Lord Suffolk, 'to use all the means which God and nature have put into our hands.' I am astonished, I am shocked, to hear such principles confessed; to hear them avowed in this country, in this House. I cannot repress my indignation—I feel myself impelled to speak. My Lords, we are called upon, as members of this House, as men, as Christians, to protest against such possible barbarity.... Such detestable principles are equally abhorrent to religion and humanity. What! To attribute the sacred sanction of God and nature to the massacres of the Indian scalping-knife! to the cannibal savage, torturing, murdering, devouring, drinking the blood of his mangled victims! Such actions shock every precept of morality, every

---

* Pro Rosc. Amer. 50, 146 sq.
† *Pro Sestio*, c. 7, 16.

sentiment of horror. These abominable principles and this most abominable avowal of them, demand the most decisive indignation."

(v) *Pity**

58. Pity is sorrow for the unhappy position of another. It presupposes love for the person affected. Therefore, in order to incline the feelings to this emotion, an effort must be made: (1) to arouse a feeling of tenderness and *interest* for the unhappy person; (2) to describe the *magnitude* of his grief, his pitiable state (e.g., poverty, loneliness, powerlessness of age, the losses suffered in possessions of mind or body, illness, persecution), by representing the evil in itself and the results of the same or other particularly saddening circumstances. (3) to excite sympathy by showing how *undeserved* and unexpected the misfortune in question is, and how nearly, through position, relation, friendship, similarity of thought, the suffering affects us; what fortitude the person has shown in misfortune, and yet how deeply he has felt it; how his misfortune may also reach us; how, perhaps, only the hearers are in a position to help him, and how this is really expected of their sympathy, etc.

Examples: Cicero's endeavour to arouse sympathy for himself by pointing out the suffering and injuries he and his have had to undergo at the hands of turbulent citizens.† See also *Pro Rosc. Amer.* 145: "Prædia mea tu possides: ego aliena misericordia . . ."; especially the treatment of the Navarchs and their parents by Verres and the execution of Gavius (de Supplic.), the perorations of the speeches *Pro Milone, Murena, Sulla, Plancio, Flacco*, in Appendix III.

Philotas, loaded with chains and accused of high treason, bewails in an affecting peroration the misfortunes of his family: "It is usual for the accused in the hour of their need to have the support of their relations. I have but lately lost two brothers; my father cannot appear, nor can I summon him, for he is accused of the same offence; he who so lately was the father of many children, may not only be robbed of his only remaining son, but may himself be laid on the funeral

---

* Arist., Rhet. 2, 8; Cic., de Inv. 1, 55-56.
† Pro. Sest. 69, 145. Cf. with this St Greg. Naz., or. 16 de Paup. Amore.

pile! Must thou, then, my beloved father, for my sake and with me die? I rob thee of life, I load with sorrow thy old age? Alas, why didst thou, against the will of the gods, give me being? Was it for such a harvest which now thou art to reap? I know not whether my youth or thy age is the more unhappy; I am cut off in the flower of my manhood, the halter will deprive thee of that life which nature would claim, if fate would but wait!"*

In similar strain Adherbal speaks before the Roman Senate about his own and his brother's unhappy lot.† This emotion is frequently met with in the poets. How touching are the words which Phocletas addresses to Neoptolemus!‡ How touching those of Andromache to Hector!§ See further the dialogue between Œdipus and the chorus.‖ Among modern orators Lally-Tollendal especially makes use of this emotion. Compare his passage on the childhood of Louis XVI.

(vi) *Shame and Remorse*

59. Shame is evoked by referring to matters which cause a man to become an object of mockery or disgrace in the eyes of his fellow-men; as, for example, words or deeds which betray a mean spirit, vulgarity, ignorance, cowardice, etc. The fault to be censured must be considered *in itself* and in its *causes*, its *circumstances* and *results;* and it must be *contrasted* and *compared* with the rectitude of others, and, especially, with the once nobler conduct of the censured person.

The feeling of shame is very strongly aroused by reminding us of such persons as formerly had a good opinion of us, whom we esteem highly, or upon whom we depend; or even of those who are much beneath us; likewise, by considerations concerning our enemies, now perhaps exulting over us; by the thought of the unworthy example we have given, how the disgrace falls upon our family, etc. In a similar way the feeling of remorse is called forth when the *sense of duty*—justice, gratitude, love—of *honour,* of neglected *ability,* is aroused, and how by our lapse from the straight path this has been debased.

* Curt. 6, 10, 30.   † Sall. Bell. Jug. c. 14.   ‡ Soph. Phil. 468-506.
§ II, 6, 429-432.   ‖ Œdip. Tyr. vv, 1297 sqq.

In this way Cicero puts to shame the Messanians who had come to Rome to praise Verres openly in spite of his innumerable former misdeeds.* The whole of the Second Philippic is full of like passages. See especially the following: "Tu istis faucibus" . . .; then, "O fœditatem hominis flagitiosam! O impudentiam, nequitiam, libidinem non ferendam (6, 15) . . ."; and "Etenim quod unquam in terris tantum flagitium exstitisse auditum est. . . . Vehebatur in essedo tribunus plebis" (c. 23, 24); in the same strain, "O audaciam immanem! Tu etiam ingredi illam domum ausus est?"† etc. The passage in *De Suppl.* in which Cicero describes the departure and the subsequent sad fate of the allied fleet, and the forcible entry of the privateers into the harbour of Syracuse is very graphic: "Egreditur . . . præclara classis in speciem, sed inops et infirma."‡ Here the dishonour inflicted on the Roman name serves to call forth indignation against Verres. See also Demosthenes§: Τούτων, ὦ ἄνδρες Αθηναῖοι, τῶν ἀνεγνωσμένων ἀληθῆ μέν ἐστι τὰ πολλὰ . . . and the passage on the present humiliation of the Athenian citizens in comparison with the position of their ancestors.‖

Massillon in his sermon on Almsdeeds gives an example of this passion. He appeals to the hard of heart as follows: "Surely, my brethren, whilst the whole country lies crushed beneath this universal scarcity; while men, created in God's image and redeemed by His Blood, like senseless beasts still the cravings of hunger with grass,¶ and, driven by direst necessity, seek in the fields for food which the earth has not produced for men, and which for them is a food unto death—surely, I say, amid all this misery you have not the heart to be the only happy ones? Whilst a whole kingdom is passing, and around your proud palaces the air is filled with groans and cries of suffering, can you, who are within, still continue to afford the same spectacle of a haughty, voluptuous life? Where then would humanity, reason, religion be? Oh, even in a heathen country you would be looked upon as wicked citizens; in every respectable circle of society as mean, despicable beings, without feeling, without generosity,

---

* Verr. iv, 11, 26, 23, 24.   † 27, 68.   ‡ 33, 86—38, 100.
§I Phil. 38.   ‖ III Olynth. 27 sqq.   ¶ At the time of the famine in 1709.

without any moral nature. For what then must you be held in the Church of Jesus Christ? For monsters, unworthy of the name of Christian which you bear; of the faith which you glory in; of the sacraments which you approach; of the holy places wherein you tread—for all these are symbols of that unity which should reign among the faithful." *

(vii) *Contempt*

60. Contempt, as Aristotle remarks, is opposed to emulation. Means contrary to those employed to arouse the latter emotion must, therefore, be made use of to awaken contempt. These means must be employed with dignity and consideration in thought and manner. The orator must understand how to discriminate between person and thing, and must not lose sight of charity; in this respect both ancient and modern orators often lamentably fail, as will be partly seen from the following examples.

Demosthenes wields this weapon against Philip. Having shown that the early Greeks would not endure even the shadow of tyranny among the Hellenes, though these in their worst excesses were true men, he goes on to prove to the Athenians how disgraceful it was to hand over their country into Philip's hands.

"If a slave or a bastard, indeed, were to waste or dissipate the property of a stranger, by Hercules! what uproar and indignation it would wring from you! But against Philip and his present conduct there is no protest at all! against him, who is not only not a Hellene, but has not even anything to do with the Greeks; no, not even is he a barbarian from a land that can be named with honour ; only a good-for-nothing Macedonian, from that land in which not even a useful slave can be bought! And yet how far is he from the culminating point of his haughtiness. Did he not, even after having destroyed the Greek towns, preside at the Pythian games?"

* It is extremely difficult to shame a person without at the same time *embittering* him ; hence treatment of this emotion requires no little oratorical tact. The orator may either include himself in the same class, as Minucius Rufus did when censuring the Roman Army (Liv. 22, 14); or he may blame in a spirit of love and kindness as Hannibal (Liv. 23, 45).

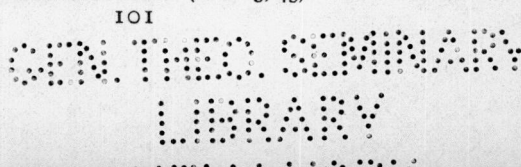

In the First Philippic he shows how contemptible the conduct of the Athenians against Philip is, in order to move them to renounce their lethargy and levity.* "Now it is of all things most laughable how we waste our opportunities. For if somebody asked you, 'Have you peace, O Athenians?' 'No, by Jupiter! not we,' someone would answer, 'We wage war with Philip.' 'Did you not choose from amongst you ten taxiarchi and strategi and phylarchi and two hipparchi? Well, what are they doing? Except a single man, whom you had to send out to the war, the others escort you in attendance on the Hieropöen in festive array. You imitate the clay-modellers; you choose taxiarchi and phylarchi for the market, not for war.'"

Compare also the caustic passage in the *De Corona* in which Demosthenes says to Æschines, and puts it into the mouth of the people to say that he is not Alexander's guest, but only his day-labourer; and the equally spirited passage of Æschines, about the sayings and doings of Demosthenes.† Cicero holds up to scorn the behaviour of Verres, who for a bribe set free the rebellious slaves, and yet such a man was honoured by his friends as a celebrated general: "What do you say, O you admirable guardian and defender of the province? Did you dare to snatch from the very jaws of death and to release slaves whom you had decided were eager to take up arms and to make war in Sicily, and whom, in accordance with the opinions of your colleagues on the bench, you had sentenced, after they had already been delivered up to punishment after the manner of our ancestors, and had been bound to the stake, in order to reserve for Roman citizens the cross which you had erected for condemned slaves? Ruined cities, when their affairs are quite desperate, are accustomed to these disastrous scenes; to have those who have been condemned released; the banished restored to their original positions; decisions which have been given rescinded. And whenever these things do take place, there is no one who is not aware that that State is hastening to its fall. O splendid general, not to be compared now to M. Aquillius, a most valiant man, but to the Paulli,

* 25, 26.   † In Ctesiph.